COLLECTED WORKS OF
C. W. VALENTINE

Volume 1

THE DIFFICULT CHILD
AND THE PROBLEM
OF DISCIPLINE

THE DIFFICULT CHILD
AND THE PROBLEM
OF DISCIPLINE

C. W. VALENTINE

Routledge
Taylor & Francis Group

LONDON AND NEW YORK

First published in 1940

This edition first published in 2015 by
Routledge
2 Park Square, Milton Park, Abingdon,
Oxfordshire, OX14 4RN
711 Third Avenue, New York, NY 10017

*Routledge is an imprint of the Taylor & Francis Group, an informa
business*

British Library Cataloguing in Publication Data
A catalogue record for this book is available from the British Library

ISBN: 978-1-138-89931-5 (Set)
ISBN: 978-1-315-69276-0 (Set) (ebk)
ISBN: 978-1-138-89937-7 (Volume 1) (hbk)
ISBN: 978-1-138-89938-4 (Volume 1) (pbk)
ISBN: 978-1-315-70790-7 (Volume 1) (ebk)

Publisher's Note
The publisher has gone to great lengths to ensure the quality of this
reprint but points out that some imperfections in the original copies
may be apparent.

Disclaimer
The publisher has made every effort to trace copyright holders and
would welcome correspondence from those they have been unable to
trace.

THE DIFFICULT CHILD
AND THE
PROBLEM OF DISCIPLINE

by

C. W. VALENTINE

METHUEN & CO. LTD., LONDON
36 Essex Street, Strand, W.C.2

This book was first published November 28th, 1940
It has been reprinted four times
Fifth edition, 1950

CATALOGUE No. 3188/U

PREFACE TO FIRST EDITION

THIS LITTLE BOOK is addressed to students of the psychology of childhood and especially of difficult children, and to parents and teachers who are trying to get from the study of psychology some light on the problems of discipline and of the difficult child. In particular I have tried to deal with some ideas which are receiving widespread attention and which masquerade as sound psychology, but which seem to be both untrue and harmful. Some of the more technical points of psychology are dealt with in footnotes, and references are given which will help the student to further reading.

After a first impulse to hold the book up until after the war, there came the realization that problems of discipline were being accentuated by the increased disorganization of education and of family life.

My thanks are due to my colleague, Mr. E. C. Cull, for kindly reading the typescript and for several useful suggestions. To Professor Cyril Burt I am greatly indebted, not only for his own extensive investigations on the psychology of children and adolescents, to which I have often referred in this book, but also for his careful reading of the proofs and for many valuable comments.

C. W. V.

PREFACE TO FOURTH EDITION

OWING to restrictions as to printing most of the additional notes and references in this edition have been placed in an Appendix. These deal with some new researches and publications which have appeared since the first edition of this book in 1940.

University of Birmingham.   C. W. V.
October, 1946.

CONTENTS

PART I

PSYCHOLOGY AND THE DIFFICULT CHILD

PART II

THE PROBLEM OF DISCIPLINE

viii THE DIFFICULT CHILD

Part One

PSYCHOLOGY AND
THE DIFFICULT CHILD

A

I

INTRODUCTION : SOME UNJUSTIFIED ASSERTIONS AS TO THE PSYCHOLOGY OF EARLY CHILDHOOD

IN THE HARD task of bringing up children in the home or in dealing with the difficult child in the school, many parents and teachers are looking to the psychologist to give guidance. Unfortunately they are apt to be bewildered by the varying doctrines of persons who adopt the label 'psychologist'. It is one aim of this book to try to sift some of these which refer to the development of children, to reveal the groundless nature of some of the dogmas, and yet to show that psychological thought can contribute something of real value in the handling of the difficult child, and in the training of normal children so that they do not *become* problem children.

It is regrettable that at present anyone without any adequate training in psychology can call himself a psychologist and even advertise himself as a consulting psychologist, with the danger of great harm being done to individuals, and certainly to the detriment of the reputation of psychology.

Such fantastic things indeed are said about the social development of children by various persons who claim the name of 'psychologist', that by some intelligent people psychology is either disliked, despised, or feared. Thus, according to a newspaper report, a speaker at a recent meeting of 'Practical Psychologists' stated that the most deadly enemy of the boy was his mother, the father coming a good second. This sweeping assertion (the speaker, according to the report, did not add 'in some cases'—which

3

might have been true) was rightly denounced by a member of the Education Committee of the City of Sheffield; but, unfortunately, he regarded it as typical of the view of psychologists, and therefore he opposed a suggestion that Local Education Authorities should engage psychologists to test and advise about children in the schools.

It is in reference to difficult or 'problem' children that such extreme and ill-founded generalizations are especially made. The term 'difficult' child here and in the title of the book, is meant to indicate not only the extreme cases of difficulty, the so-called 'problem' children who are in complete revolt against authority at home and at school, or who play truant or lie or steal, but in particular that much more frequent type which is 'difficult' at home or at school, resentful of discipline, or excessively aggressive; the type of child who in the last century would have been called simply the 'naughty' or 'spoilt' child. We shall also refer to the child who is excessively diffident and needs encouragement rather than restraint, and to the child who becomes too emotionally dependent.

It is significant of the change of attitude that such 'naughty' children should now be studied as 'problems', and the causes of their naughtiness sought in their environment and training rather than merely in their 'original sin'. We shall see reason to think, however, that this attribution of the causes of all naughtiness to training or environment has gone too far; that we cannot ignore the great element of truth in the idea that there are inborn defects in varying degrees. We shall see also that some popular dogmatic assertions so readily accepted by many parents and teachers, are not justified by our present knowledge of the social psychology of early childhood.

Gaps in our knowledge of the social psychology of childhood

It is true that great advances have been made recently in the study of intelligence and of some special abilities in childhood: but when we come to consider the early development of character and disposition we find much greater difficulty in stating general facts. True, we have many reports on the characteristics of children of different ages: and much evidence on individual differences in temperament even in the earliest years.[1] So cautious a writer as Professor Cyril Burt, on the basis of his own wide experience of school children and juvenile delinquents, concludes that 'to a large extent, the behaviour of the child who is temperamentally subnormal resembles that of a child who is considerably younger than himself'.[2] But as to the very young child we have little knowledge as to what is really normal or at least 'desirable' and what we should regard as a bad sign for future development. Rapid conformity to adult standards (often taken as the ideal) may not be essential for later normal development.

The hasty application of insecure psychological theories as to standards of normal or healthy conduct will only bring scepticism, ridicule, and perhaps reaction. A recent visitor to an American Nursery School found a mother greatly upset because of a report on her three-year-old boy, which said he was 'lacking in co-operation and leadership' and that 'concentration was somewhat spasmodic'! The mother was distressed because the boy was not 'socially conscious'—and this at three years! Generally speaking, the test of character

---

[1] For a summary of these (especially of Austrian and American results) see Charlotte Bühler's article, 'The Social Behaviour of Children', in *A Handbook of Child Psychology*, edited by Carl Murchison. See also Katherine Bridges' *Social and Emotional Development of the Pre-School Child*. [2] *The Subnormal Mind*, p. 326.

at this early age seemed to be: 'How far does it approximate to that of an adult?' I suggest that we do not know enough at present to say whether it is not as good, or even better, for a boy of four or five to be modest and retiring rather than attempt leadership; or whether at ten or twelve he should not be somewhat aggressive instead of too peaceful or obedient. As Claparéde has pointed out, it will not hasten the development of the tadpole into a frog if we cut off its tail.

We need especially much fuller and more exact knowledge of what may be the characteristics of a normal child and what are the signs of later abnormal social or emotional development, needing exceptional treatment. Within my own family circle I can cite the following examples of apparent excessive emotional outbursts in early years which were disturbing at the time, but were succeeded by satisfactory development later without any special 'treatment'.

(1) Occasional violent tempers in one of our boys at the age of 2;0 to 2;6[1]—at times rolling on the ground with rage—sometimes it seemed merely through frustration of his wishes. This proved consistent with development into an exceptionally equable temperament in young manhood.

(2) Hysterical night fears (seeing 'horrid faces', etc.) in one of our little girls at about 3;0—very troublesome over a considerable period; these proved consistent not only with a marked stability of emotion later, but with an unusual absence of fears of all kinds—darkness, animals, rough seas, burglars, and with a passion for aeroplane flying. Yet I find that the director of a Child Guidance Clinic declares that night fears are a sign of a 'nervous' child!

(3) An outburst of violent temper in another girl was noted at about 2;6, in which she struck a maid with a

---

[1] Here and later I use the common method to indicate years and months; thus 2;6 means 2 years and 6 months.

knife and afterwards boasted, 'I did bleed her!' Yet this girl grew up to be extremely sympathetic to pain in other people and in animals.

Rage, cruelty, hysterical fears *may* certainly appear at various stages in the development of healthy, happy and intelligent children. One investigation indeed suggests that a difficult period of revolt against discipline—between the ages of 2;0 and 4;0 is usually a good sign. H. Helzer for example reports that of 100 such children, 84 developed later normally as to 'will': while of 100 who had no such period of revolt, only 26 developed normally, the others revealing feeble wills.[1]

As to children of school age, say from 6 to 14 or from 11 to 18, the teacher of long experience has a fairly good idea as to what type of behaviour is usual, though it may be limited to behaviour in school, and largely to behaviour under the particular teacher's own influence. But even here we cannot assume that 'good' behaviour in school is necessarily a condition for, or a certain indicator of, a normal healthy or vigorous personality in manhood.

In particular we are uncertain as to the extent to which various types of character or behaviour are due to heredity, or environment, are inborn or acquired. Consider such tendencies as self-assertion or submissiveness, affection, suggestibility or stubbornness, sympathy or aggression. We have at present no accurate means of estimating the strength of such tendencies or the degree to which these are inborn, or dependent on or modified by experience. Consequently on these matters ideas tend to be much looser than our ideas about intelligence, more extreme views are expressed, and fads flourish.

We shall consider in Chapter II some unproved assump-

[1] *Zeit. für pädagogische Psychologie*, 1929, p. 83. Quoted by J. Abramson in *L'Enfant et L'Adolescent Instables*, p. 255 (Paris, 1940).

tions about the question of heredity and environment, especially the assumption often made that abnormal conduct is almost invariably due to social environment or wrong training.

The supposed significance of sex problems in infancy

Psycho-analysts are sometimes responsible for sweeping and unproved assertions about children, and unfortunately in the minds of many people psycho-analysis is identified with psychology. We shall see later in the chapters on discipline how some extreme ideas and modern fads as to discipline are due largely to speculative dogmas of certain psycho-analysts or a misunderstanding of some of their sound ideas. Some of their assertions about the emotional development of little children are supported only by most flimsy evidence. No doubt many readers, whether parents or teachers, have been faced with the statement that the main difficulties of discipline, the chief cause of defiance or of excessive fears in the child and of early conflicts in the home, are in some way connected with sex. Some parents having read such statements have reported that they were afraid of showing affection towards their children for fear of stimulating an unholy sex impulse in them! We had better say something about this bogey of infantile sexuality at the start.[1]

[1] Psycho-analysts, when their views on the importance of sex in childhood are criticized, sometimes retort that their critics are prejudiced against Freud's views and that they are revolted by frank discussion of sex-problems, and so forth. Perhaps therefore I might mention here that years ago, when Freud's ideas were not so widely known in this country, I wrote a book (*The New Psychology of the Unconscious*) which I hoped would introduce more students to a knowledge of his work. Furthermore, one reason why I deplore the far-fetched and exaggerated statements (as they seem to me) about the influence of sex factors in early childhood, is that they will tend to cause contempt for all Freud's teachings and so lessen attention to the serious problems of sex in early manhood or early womanhood, to which his work lends added

Stress on the influence of the early development of sex in children has led in some quarters to some fantastic explanations of their behaviour. Melanie Klein, for example, who attempts to psycho-analyse little children even of three or four, thus describes her treatment of a little girl of three and three-quarter years of age, said to be neurotic. The girl, when playing with a toy man and cart, threw the man out of the cart, and Mrs. Klein explained to the child that she did this because she resented the father's sexual relations with her mother, which Mrs. Klein apparently described in detail to the child. That child had been troublesome at home, and Mrs. Klein gives *as evidence of the correctness of her interpretation*, the fact that the little girl was now more friendly to her and wanted to come to her playroom again the next week. Of course! Who else would tell her such wonderful fairy stories?

Now Melanie Klein may not have much influence on education, but such a well-known writer as Dr. Susan Isaacs thinks so well of Mrs. Klein's opinions and methods, that she dedicates one of her own books to her with the words: 'To Melanie Klein who understands the minds of children'; and Dr. Isaacs herself attributes so much influence to sex in infancy that she states that 'idiosyncracies about food, and difficulties as to training in cleanliness are mainly the outcome of deep-seated mental conflict connected with sexual life'.[1]

significance. The extreme and unscientific views of some medical psychologists also prejudice many medical men against psychology in general and medical psychology in particular. This is especially unfortunate in view of the great contributions to psychology made by such men as McDougall, Rivers, C. S. Myers, Bernard Hart and others in this country, and of the valuable work now being done by medical men who have learned much from the modern psychology of the unconscious, without adopting Freud's views *in toto*.

[1] *Social Development in Young Children*, p. 15. The main body of Dr. Isaacs' admirable contributions to practical methods for the education of young children seems to me to be quite independent of her ideas on the great significance of sex in infancy.

To deal adequately with the supposed evidence of sexuality in infancy is not possible in this brief book. I hope to examine it more fully in a book to be published shortly.[1]

We may consider, however, some other types of evidence in addition to that just exemplified.

One common fallacy is the assumption that early interest in and curiosity about the sex organs, imply the beginnings of the development of sex proper. Of course the infant is naturally interested in all parts of his body, and becomes more so when he finds differences between himself and his sister. This curiosity is often stimulated by prohibition against exploration. Indeed I once roused enormous curiosity in my four children—whose ages at the time of the experiment ranged from three to twelve—simply by telling them that a certain box (which was in fact empty) must not be opened. Repeated questioning about the box by the children continued for days, and with the youngest for some weeks.

No doubt when there is persistent or intense interest in the sex apparatus, even after normal curiosity should have been satisfied, there is possibly some premature and excessive development of sex in the child. But in most families still, I imagine, natural curiosity is far from fully satisfied.

A second type of evidence of sex development in early childhood offered by some psycho-analysts, is the fact that mere infants of one or two years will play with their genitals, and masturbation may sometimes be persistent through later infancy. But a normal baby of one or two loves to handle and play with anything within reach. He begins with his own fingers, nose, hair, toes, and so on, and the genitals naturally come in for some examination. Even granting that such repeated playing of this kind suggests a pleasure more decided than that gained in playing with hands and feet,

[1] Probably under the title 'Mental Development in Early Childhood', or 'Foundations of Child Psychology'.

there is no ground for supposing that pleasure to be intense, except in the smaller number of abnormal cases which have been observed: and even in such cases there is no evidence that it is accompanied by any traces of the sex impulse proper, though it may well be a sign of precocity and exceptional strength of the sex impulse later.

The supposed Oedipus Complex

As to the Oedipus complex—the supposed desire (conscious or unconscious) of the boy of only two or three to 'possess' the mother, and the consequent jealous hatred for the father (or of the girl for the mother), the sweeping generalizations made by Freud on this are based on most inadequate direct evidence, so far as reported, of a few cases and on the results of the psycho-analysis of adults, though Freud himself later declared that the complex disappears in normal adults.

Freud asserts that from 'direct observation of children . . . it is easy to see that the little man wants his mother all to himself', and 'shows his satisfaction when the father goes away'; while the little girl feels 'a need to do away with the superfluous mother and to take her place'.[1]

In order to gather evidence on this and other matters concerning sex development in infancy I submitted questions about the early development of their own children to fifteen friends, nearly all teachers of psychology or former advanced students of mine in psychology. Reports on their children during the first few years (the number varying from about 50 children reported on at ages 2;0 – 3;0 and decreasing to about 30 infants of 3;0 – 4;0 and 25 at 5;0 – 6;0) were made confidentially by the father and mother in collaboration; they are in direct conflict with the assertions of

[1] See *Lectures on Psycho-Analysis*, pp. 279–280.

Freud about the increasing dislike of little boys for the father after 2;0, or the jealousy of little girls of their mothers.

As one might expect, the mothers are judged to be decidedly preferred by the majority of both boys and girls up to at least 7;0 or 8;0. As to sex differences, so far as they do appear it is the girls rather than the boys who especially prefer the mothers, even during the years supposed to be particularly critical for the Oedipus complex. These direct observations of children also conflict with Freud's statements about the jealousy of a child felt towards one of the parents, though often a child is jealous of another child.[1]

Fallacies about the signs of abnormality and with respect to evidence

There is another type of fallacious argument for which we must be on the watch in considering problems of normal and abnormal conduct and especially the signs of abnormality.

[1] Some psycho-analysts no doubt would reply: 'Oh, but deep in the unconscious the attitude of the children would be different. You could only find that by analysis.' But it should be noted that Freud has claimed that the 'direct observation of children' shows these phenomena; they are 'easy to see'. (See his *Lectures on Psycho-Analysis*, p. 279.)

Some psycho-analysts would base the doctrine of the Oedipus complex or such ideas as repressed infantile homosexuality almost entirely on the results of analysis of adults. Now while I fully agree that free association or word association tests may lead us back to genuine experiences which have been forgotten (and have myself indeed made use of both such methods in dealing with persons sent to me for analysis), it must be emphasized that any series of associations if sufficiently prolonged is bound in the long run to introduce some ideas of sex—indeed very quickly when the patient knows that the analyst is on the lookout especially for sex. That very knowledge will suggest ideas of sex to him. One of the leading psycho-analysts when analysing another medical psychologist was afterwards stated by the latter to appear very bored during most of the series of associations but to sit up and take keen notice when terms of sex appeared!

For an acute criticism of the doctrine of the Oedipus complex see William McDougall's *Psycho-analysis and Social Psychology*, especially Appendix IV.

Consider for example the assertions made by some medical psycho-analysts who have found a number of difficult or neurotic children showing certain characteristics or habits, say thumb-sucking or violent temper-tantrums. There is a tendency to say that these symptoms are associated with some misconduct or nervous trouble of the child or adult *without any enquiry as to how frequently these same traits are found in normal children.* For example, Freud himself connects habitual or perverse kissing in adults with excessive thumb-sucking in infancy; in the men there is a marked desire for drinking and smoking, while, as to women, he says: 'Many of my female patients showing disturbances in eating, choking sensations and vomiting, have been energetic thumb-suckers during infancy.'[1] He does not refer to the possibility of, let us say, half the number of *normal* children being thumb-suckers of this kind; in which case, of course, it would be likely that half his patients would have been thumb-suckers in childhood, without there being any connection whatever between the two things. As a matter of fact, a recent enquiry in which sixty 'problem children', ages 2;0 to 6;0 and sixty normal children of similar ages in a nursery school were compared, gave the following results. Out of the sixty problem children, twenty-six were thumb-suckers; among the normal group, who were causing no difficulty, twenty-eight were also thumb-suckers. So thumb-sucking was found in nearly half the children, and was rather more frequent among the normal children.[2]

Again, in a recent book, a medical psychologist gives the impression that, because some neurotic children have been excessively conscientious at an early age, therefore the over-

---

[1] *Three Contributions to the Theory of Sex*, p. 45 (New York).
[2] See W. W. Blatz and J. D. M. Griffin, *An Evaluation of the Case Histories of a Group of Pre-School Children*, p. 10 (University of Toronto Press, 1936).

conscientious child is 'really presenting signs of illness'. Else-where Freud himself utters a warning against such illogical reversals as this. He writes: 'Signs of childhood neuroses can be detected in all adult neurotics . . . *but by no means all children who show these signs become neurotic in later life.*'[1]

As a further example of the danger of interpreting symp-toms as abnormal I may give the results of an enquiry as to Compulsive Obsessions—tendencies to carry out repeatedly useless or meaningless actions, with the feeling that one *must* do so. I once heard a leading authority on Child Guidance work state that he took a certain obsession which troubled a girl (viz. the feeling that she must count the windows in every room she went into) as partial evidence that she was neurotic or abnormal in some way. Having noted a number of such obsessions in children whom I did not think abnormal, I felt sceptical about this and I made an enquiry among three classes each of about one hundred graduate students. With very few exceptions they all reported that they had experienced such compulsions at one time or another: yet practically all of these students were sufficiently stable to carry on the difficult work of school teaching satisfactorily. Several children I have known intimately were considerably troubled by such compulsions in later child-

---

[1] See *Inhibitions, Symptoms and Anxiety*, p. 127. The medical man referred to above also asserts that if a mother fusses too much over a child's bowel routine, the child is in danger of developing into an over-moral adult. He gives no evidence for this. How many cases indeed can a doctor follow from infancy to adulthood? or if the assertion is based on enquiry, how reliable can the mother's report be as to whether years ago she so 'fussed'; and how many mothers so fuss *without* the child's becoming over-moral; and how many children are 'over-moral' without such fussing; or are mothers who over-fuss about bowels also over-fussy about morals and so make the children over-moral? and so on. It will be seen that it would be extremely difficult to establish the fact of such a tendency. Yet it is asserted as an actual danger by this writer; see the chapter by Dr. Clifford Allen in *The Growing Child and its Problems*, edited by Emanuel Miller (London, 1937), p. 118.

hood (e.g. repeatedly shutting and re-shutting a door, or even attempting to trace a Greek Key pattern with the movement of the tongue!): yet they grew up to be exceptionally well-balanced and stable in temperament and character. Parents and teachers, therefore, need not be unduly alarmed at the occasional occurrence of such compulsions in the child, though the persistence of one dominant type of compulsion may sometimes be the sign of an outlet for a repressed impulse.[1]

Some psycho-analysts of the type we have just mentioned seem to have little sense of evidence and frequently write as though they had hardly ever come into contact with normal children. A few coincidences seem to be enough to provide convincing evidence to them. Examples of this appear sometimes in the interpretation of children's drawings. Thus if a child draws a circle it is said to be a sex-symbol (it can conveniently serve for male or female); if he draws a cylindrical shape it is a male sex-symbol—if oval a female sex-symbol; or if the particular trouble of the child is known, how easy it is to read something appropriately symbolical into a given picture.

A recondite explanation of actions seems sometimes actually to be preferred to an obvious one. In the collection of essays already mentioned, another writer, referring to the value and interest of certain kinds of play, for example with water, says that 'water corresponds to the deepest and most primitive needs of the child'. Yes, but surely water is also a unique kind of material to play with; and would quicksilver be enjoyed any the less if it were available? Yet another medical man writes that the reason why some children are so prone to accidents is that they have an inner tendency to self-punishment or pain-seeking![2]

---

[1] See C. Burt: *The Subnormal Mind*, pp. 268 ff.
[2] *The Growing Child and its Problems*, p. 160.

Some educators who are very much in the public eye, also make sweeping generalizations with a minimum basis of facts. Mr. A. S. Neill, for example, in his recent book, *That Dreadful School*, in which he describes his own school, states (p. 77) that he is convinced that 'trouser-messing' is in 'every case' due to hatred against the mother for the starving of love. He is confident of this, although he adds that he has had only about one example of this kind in fifteen years! Similarly he repeatedly stated, without giving proof, that he is convinced that a great many misdemeanours of boys, including what most of us would call moral delinquency, would be done away with if we could remove what he calls the 'masturbation verbot'.

No doubt speculation and hypothesis have their rightful place in the development of psychological knowledge: but let us distinguish between that and real knowledge, and not turn hypothesis into dogma. Those who are looking for guidance in the treatment of difficult children should perpetually ask 'what is the evidence for this assertion?', however able the orator who makes it, however eminent (in physical matters) the doctor who supports a particular view of psycho-therapy, however successful in practice the teacher who attributes his success to some particular theory —not allowing for the effect of his own personality, or, if he is the head of a private school, for the peculiar selection of pupils his own eccentricities may attract.

In particular we must learn to distinguish between the sound element of truth in a given doctrine, and the error of its extreme form—as in the dogma that the first few years are decisive for character, and as in several ideas about discipline, topics which we shall discuss in later chapters. Similarly we must guard against the danger of generalizing about all children on the basis of the study of children under certain conditions (as in some modern views about the necessity for nursery or kindergarten schools for all children between the years 2 – 5), and with respect to particular methods which seem to have been useful in the treatment of certain problem children in Child Guidance Clinics, topics which again we shall discuss in later chapters.

II

ARE THERE NO PROBLEM CHILDREN, ONLY PROBLEM PARENTS? HEREDITY *VERSUS* ENVIRONMENT

Inborn individual differences

The idea that character is entirely determined by early training and environment, and that all abnormalities of conduct are due to wrong treatment, is often implied and sometimes explicitly asserted by writers of the type we have been considering. 'There are no problem children,' it has been said, 'only problem parents.' I have noted this general attitude in some half-dozen books I have recently reviewed, written by medical men especially for parents.

Such assertions are liable to have unfortunate results, especially when made with the prestige which is apt to be attached to a medical man even when he speaks about mental processes. Some conscientious parents are beginning to worry unduly lest their own way of bringing up a child must be entirely responsible for all his undisciplined behaviour; some enthusiastic educationists are claiming that, if only teachers dealt wisely with the children at the earlier stages, we should have no difficult children later on. Certainly this idea is prominent in much recent psychoanalytic literature and especially in the teaching of Adler and his followers about the social development of young children, which refers almost exclusively to the influence of *environment* in producing unsocial conduct or abnormal emotional outbursts.

It is especially surprising that some medical psychologists pay so little attention to what is, after all, a plain biological fact, namely, the fact of inborn individual variations. For example, if there is too great aggressiveness or stubbornness shown by the child, one has to consider whether this is due, not to the home environment or repression in school, but rather to excessively strong, innate aggressiveness or self-assertion in the child himself.

We know that nature allows enormous individual variations in innate intelligence and even in vital physical functions. There are, indeed, extreme inborn defects in such essential parts as the brain, abnormalities in organs so essential to life as the heart and some important glands, which may lead to death within a few days of birth. If such variations still occur in functions so important for life itself —useless and dangerous variations which even the passing of countless generations, in which such variations have proved fatal, has failed to eliminate, can we put any limit to the extent to which nature allows variations in far less important matters—for example, self-assertion and self-submission, anger, fear, affection, suggestibility and so forth? Individual differences in such traits have indeed been observed in the first year or two of life, among children brought up almost from birth in the same institution. The evidence of unlike twins brought up from birth in the same home is still more weighty. Even the Dionne Quins—biologically similar (like similar twins) and brought up in the same nursery—show by the age of two years marked individual differences in their social development.[1]

We have, then, both presumptive and direct evidence which makes extremely improbable the causation of *all* differences in such traits by differences of environment— parental upbringing, school discipline, etc.

---

[1] See *Collected Studies of the Dionne Quintuplets* (Section 3) (Univ. of Toronto Press, 1937). As to twins see N. D. M. Hirsch, *Twins: Heredity and Environment*, especially Chap. 9 (Harvard Univ. Press, 1930).

Bad environment surmounted by many

Again, in spite of certain clear correlations between (*a*) delinquency, or undisciplined conduct, or neurotic tendencies, and (*b*) certain types of adverse environment, we know that many children survive such an environment without disaster.

Among the 200 juvenile delinquents studied by Professor Burt, about 58 per cent of the delinquents came from 'defective' homes, *but so did about 26 per cent of the non-delinquents*.[1] Also, 39 per cent of the delinquents came from homes not characterized by defective discipline: while of the homes of the non-delinquents, 6 per cent were 'vicious' and 12 per cent ill-disciplined. Bad environment, then, does not seem to be always enough to cause delinquency, any more than satisfactory home conditions ensure its absence. This is still more strongly supported by the main fact that not all the brothers and sisters of delinquents are themselves delinquents.

Similar evidence to Burt's is given by an American investigator, Dr. N. D. Hirsch. He argues indeed that 'broken homes' are themselves largely due to the poor constitutional make-up of the parents, which tends to be transmitted to the children.[2]

This is a fair counterweight to the suggestion that in some of the apparently 'good' homes where a delinquent or problem child appears there may be psychological difficulties not apparent to the social investigator. I should agree; and am content if the critic concludes that in individual cases we cannot be quite certain whether innate or environmental factors are more important. What I am

---

[1] See *The Young Delinquent*, by Cyril Burt, 1925, p. 53, p. 64 and p. 101. Note that not all the items under 'Defective Family Relationships' in Burt's Table IV are types of 'broken homes'.

[2] See his *Dynamic Causes of Juvenile Crimes* (Cambridge, Massachusetts).

contending against is the dogmatic assertion that all delinquents or difficult children are such entirely because of bad environment or training.

The Inheritance of Temperamental Traits

We might support Hirsch's contention by similar presumptive arguments to those we have used above. Thus there is a large amount of evidence in favour of hereditary influences on intelligence: not merely the decided correlations in ordinary families between the intelligence of children and that of their parents, but the appearance of such correlations when the children have been separated from their parents and brought up in institutions: also the great variations in the intelligence of children of different parents brought up from early infancy in the same homes, the high frequency of the appearance of mental deficiency or dullness among the parents or other near relatives of mental defectives, and so on. If there are such decided hereditary influences on intelligence it is surely highly probable that there would be similar influences on temperamental traits, particularly when these are the outcome of physico-chemical factors (excitability of the nervous system and of the glands of internal secretion). Thus Burt on the basis of his own investigations, and other evidence, concluded that the 'primary emotions related to instincts' were more dependent on inheritance than even intellectual processes are. (See his article 'The Inheritance of Mental Characters' in the *Eugenics Review*, Vol. 4.)

There would be general agreement, however, that the development of moral characteristics—including the modification and co-ordination of temperamental traits—can be profoundly affected by environmental influences.[1]

[1] On the inheritance of mental traits in man see L. H. Snyder, *The Principles of Heredity*, chap. 27 (London and New York, 1935); C. Burt,

*Innate defects in juvenile delinquents and
problem children*

Burt, in his cautious examination of the rich results of
his enquiry on Juvenile Delinquents, came to the conclusion
that nearly half of the 200 delinquents had 'profound and
widespread instability of emotions' *as an inborn defect*;
whereas this was true of only 10 per cent of his non-delinquent control group. He finally concludes that some *innate*
factor was the major cause of delinquency in 36 per cent of
the boys and 41 per cent of the girls (p. 605). Burt also
points out that Healey, dealing in his American enquiries
with more hardened offenders, found environmental influences playing the decisive part in only 25 per cent of his cases.

Hirsch rightly stresses the fact that only 22 per cent of
the brothers and sisters of his 600 young delinquents were
themselves delinquents. Also relevant are the facts gathered
by W. Healey and A. Bronner as to 105 delinquents and
105 of their brothers and sisters, who were not delinquents.
The most striking differences were found under the heading
of 'personality characteristics', especially as to hyperactivity
and restlessness; in this 68 of the delinquents exceeded the
corresponding control and only 11 were less active. In 25
of the delinquents (against 2 of the non-delinquents) there
were 'personality' deviations involving a lack of 'normal
inhibitory powers'.[1] The Report of a 'follow-up' study of

The Subnormal Mind, pp. 72 ff. (on the causes of mental deficiency), and
The Backward Child, p. 446, and other Index references; Evelyn M.
Lawrence, *An Investigation into the Relation Between Intelligence and
Inheritance* (Cambridge, 1931); a discussion of enquiries bearing on the
eugenic aspect of this question is given by E. J. G. Bradford in an
article, 'The Relation of Intelligence to Varying Birth Rate in Different
Social Grades' (*British Journal of Educational Psychology*, Vol. VII, 1937).

[1] See *New Light on Delinquency and its Treatment* (Yale Univ. Press,
1936), pp. 58, 63, 76. Perhaps on the other hand we should mention
the fact that 28 of the delinquents against 8 of the controls had suffered
from 'many severe illnesses' (p. 57).

500 children treated at the Tavistock Clinic, made at least three years after treatment was finished, states that 'some children recover in the face of apparently insuperable difficulties, and some retain their symptoms for reasons which often remain obscure'.[1]

In the enquiry already referred to in Chapter I, in which 60 problem children were compared with 60 normal children, it was found that the most marked of all the differences in the environments of the two groups was that of 'faulty discipline', found in the homes of 38 of the problem children but only 8 of the normal. Yet supremely important as discipline is, even this left 37 per cent of the problem children coming from homes when the discipline seemed wise, and 13 per cent of the normal children under bad discipline without succumbing.

Too sweeping generalizations have also been made about the special danger of being an only child, or the eldest or the youngest child. The assertions of Alfred Adler, for example, about the consequences of being the eldest or youngest of the family are not supported by most recent enquiries.[2] These enquiries give varying results, as we may expect when the groups dealt with are small and their investigators different: but they suggest, when taken together, that in different families and with different dispositions in the various children, the special difficulties of being the eldest or youngest or middle child will vary greatly. Furthermore they show that the dangers of being an only child, though

---

[1] See the *Tavistock Clinic Report for 1938*, p. 21.

[2] See the summary of a considerable number of recent researches given by Charlotte Bühler in her article on 'The Social Behaviour of Children' in *A Handbook of Child Psychology*, edited by Carl Murchison (2nd edition), p. 402. The conflicting nature of the evidence, the difficulties of proper statistical treatment, and the danger of obscuring the complexity of causes, are also stressed by H. E. Jones in the same volume in his article on 'The Order of Birth'.

no doubt considerable with certain types of parents and children, have sometimes been greatly exaggerated.

Summing up as to congenital factors and environmental influences, the facts suggest: (*a*) that the social development of a certain proportion of children will be fairly satisfactory whatever the difficulties of environment; (*b*) that the development of some others will be abnormal even in good surroundings—at least until we learn better how to deal with them; while (*c*) there remains another group (probably much the largest group) of border-line children who cannot resist the influence of bad environment, yet may develop satisfactorily in a good environment. In our present state of knowledge we cannot say precisely what proportion that border-line group is, or how to detect them with certainty at an early age.

Put in another way, we may expect that some children will, at least at an early age, be excessively aggressive and cruel, or selfish or ill-tempered, whatever their early treatment may be: while others may be neglected and even ill-treated at home and yet remain honest, kindly, sympathetic and unselfish.

All this of course is no justification for neglecting the bad environment or training of any child, however much his defects seem to be innate. We must always hope that some wiser treatment or better surroundings will cause improvement. But the facts do not allow us to attribute *all* failures to bad environment or mistaken discipline alone: though some day increased knowledge of child psychology, the ability to detect weaknesses in the child at a very early age, and greater experience in varying kinds of discipline or other treatment for different types of children, may help us to improve those cases of marked congenital defects which at present appear even in what seems to us the best environment and under the wisest kind of discipline.

III

IS CHARACTER DETERMINED IN THE EARLY YEARS? THE CASE FOR THE KINDERGARTEN OR THE NURSERY SCHOOL

Inadequate evidence of early fixation of character

Another unsubstantiated doctrine is that the future development of the child is already fixed in the first half dozen years or less. True, the increasing importance attached in recent times to proper training in the earliest years is a welcome development, and the view that every mother knows instinctively how best to bring up her child at least during infancy is held now by few except perhaps by some mothers themselves.

We are not questioning the view that training in the first five or six years is supremely important for the development of character. Here, again, however, the great element of truth in an idea has been exaggerated. Freud, for example, has stated that 'the little human being is often a finished product in his fourth or fifth year'.[1] Adler went even further and seems to have thought the first few months might be decisive.[2] Now, it is true that psycho-analysts have shown that profound emotional experiences in early years may continue to exert an influence on the child when he grows up, although he may have forgotten those experiences. Further, if bad social relationships are set up between the child and the parent in these first years, it may be impossible in many cases to change these relationships later on, even though the child's character has matured consider-

[1] *Introductory Lectures on Psycho-Analysis,* 1921, p. 298.
[2] See *Understanding Human Nature,* p. 42. Adler's view is all the stranger because he minimizes the influence of heredity on character. *Op. cit.,* p. 23.

ably, and he may now be disposed to behave quite differently towards other people. Incidentally, that is probably one of the reasons why children at a later stage, especially at adolescence, are often ready to be influenced by some persons other than their parents, because they can start afresh, and the antagonism 'fixated' upon a parent is not felt towards the new individual.

What the psycho-analysts, however, have not proved is that it is impossible for children with an unfortunate social training in the very earliest years to improve later and perhaps to recover completely from any of these effects. Some of the psycho-analysts, indeed, themselves supply excellent examples of the way in which such recovery has taken place; and most of the beneficial results of child guidance work surely indicate that such early disadvantages are not irremediable—even among the worst examples. Apart from any special psychological treatment, the mere transference of problem children to a new environment often has a marked effect, as we shall see in the next chapter.

The great changes that sometimes takes place at adolescence for good or evil are further examples to the point. I add 'or evil', for occasionally changes may even occur in that direction; Adler himself cites the case of a girl who was a 'model child up to the time she was ten years old', but gravely deteriorated later.[1] As to less extreme cases, the records of Children's Homes and Reformatory Schools, and even of the Nursery Schools, show that the character of a child may be decidedly changed when he is moved to a new environment. Decided changes are also often noted in children who enter an infant school at 5;0 or 6;0 when the home environment has been unsatisfactory.[2]

---

[1] See *The Education of Children*, p. 140.

[2] Dr. Susan Isaacs, herself a good Freudian, testifies to this: see her section of *The Educational Guidance of the School Child*, p. 68.

Nevertheless, we must admit the possibility that bad influences in these first five or six years, or wrong discipline —whether too severe or too lax—may have effects which in some children, perhaps in most, cannot be entirely eradicated later: and surely here it is wiser to act upon a possibility, even if confident generalizations cannot yet be made. Certainly, when home conditions are bad, we should try either to improve them or to introduce the child to some better environment as early as possible lest he should be turned into a 'difficult' or 'problem' child.

The case for the Nursery School

The conviction as to the great importance of the early years has been the main source of two valuable institutions of recent years, namely, the Nursery School and the Child Guidance Clinic. Two main ideas underlie these two movements. (*a*) It is being more widely recognized that the school cannot be expected to do all it could for the character of the child if he only comes under the school's influence at the age of 5 or 6; hence the advocacy of the Nursery School for the years 2 to 5. (*b*) Further, it is also being recognized that we cannot expect the school alone to do everything to make the aggressive unsociable boy into a decent co-operative citizen, that the school must have the help of the home, and if family influences seem harmful, we must try to modify them.[1] This is the main idea behind the Child Guidance Movement.

My own view is that these two main ideas, (*a*) and (*b*), may be accepted as fundamental principles for general guidance. The importance of the home influence in the

---

[1] To improve home conditions is a difficult and in some cases an impossible task. Yet intelligent parents can sometimes be led to see the wrongness of their treatment of a child, their methods of discipline, etc., as we shall see later.

majority of cases, the frequency with which 'problem children' come from 'broken homes', the effects of faulty discipline, or the bad example of the parents—all these are indicated, not only by such evidence as we have mentioned in the last chapter, but by evidence gathered in Child Guidance Clinics, in spite of the fact that innate disposition seems to be in many cases the chief cause of good or bad character. For this evidence I would refer readers to recent annual reports of the London, Birmingham or Bath Clinics.[1] A great proportion of the extremely difficult children come from 'broken homes', where one parent is dead, or the father has deserted the mother, etc. For example, out of the two hundred and twelve children treated recently in the Birmingham Clinic, about 46 per cent came from such homes. Others, as we know, are being brought up in homes where one parent is perpetually drunk, or occasionally in prison, or where there is some great weakness in discipline —extreme violence or extreme laxity, or where one parent is indulgent and the other over-severe, or where there is perpetual strife between parents.[2]

It seems clear that in such cases, even though some of the children develop fairly well, thanks largely to the influence of the infant school, others grow beyond the capacity of the ordinary school to deal with. They need a new environment for special treatment, and, in some cases, a careful psychological examination, to discover the fundamental causes of their abnormal conduct. Here is work more than enough for our existing clinics.

Similarly, it does not need, I think, a prolonged enquiry to come to the conclusion that the nursery school is justi-

[1] Also to a recent book by C. Rogers, *The Clinical Treatment of the Problem Child.*

[2] That this last condition may be worse than a 'broken home' is the conclusion of Dr. Rogers after a survey of various investigations. *Op. cit.*, p. 181.

fying its existence in the poorest quarters of our cities. Some of the children are living in the homes of the kinds just mentioned; others at least in homes in which the mother has to go out to work to supplement the family income. Some are in even more adverse environments. May I give two or three brief examples taken from one small nursery school known to me?

(i) *Rupert*—age, three years. Has no mother; his eldest brother of nine years is reported to go often to the public house late in evening to get his father to come home and put Rupert to bed.

(ii) *Augustus*—age, three and a half; often seen playing on the steps of the public house late at night waiting for both his mother and father to come out. Uses picture film captions in his games: says to the teacher as he raises his glass of milk, 'Happy days, Miss— I'm 'aving me 'alf pint—'alf a pint of whiskey!'

(iii) *Eveline*—age, between three and four. Obviously disliked by the mother, who is constantly criticizing her and revealing her dislike in the presence of the child. A baby brother has recently been born.

The physical and social conditions, then, of some homes are strong reasons for placing the little children in nursery schools, whatever may be thought about the need for intellectual education at this early stage. Even among devoted parents some are hopelessly ignorant, not only of how to feed little children, but still more frequently of how to deal with them. Some children, even before the age of five, are allowed to become domineering; some under violent discipline become repressed and highly nervous.

The nursery schools can report cases in which little children, who have been extremely difficult on admission, appear almost different personalities after a few weeks in the school environment. That this is not due merely to the child becoming more mature, is suggested by two things: first, the suddenness with which the change sometimes takes place; and, second, the fact that the child's conduct, though changed at school, may continue on old lines at home.

The purposes of the Nursery School and the Child Guidance Clinic are by no means disconnected, though their connection has not been sufficiently emphasized. Just as medicine generally has become more and more preventive and the State itself has taken the leading part in preventing the spread of disease, so, in the social education of the young children, we must surely become more 'preventive'. The earlier detection and, if possible, the side-tracking of abnormal aggressiveness and other anti-social attitudes in the Nursery School, may reduce the number of obstinate cases of problem children who come to the Child Guidance Clinic so late that improvement comes only very slowly and sometimes, perhaps, never at all.

In spite, however, of all these advantages of the Nursery School for children from bad homes, we have as yet no proof that a Nursery School or Kindergarten is essential for the proper training of every child from two to five years. The kindergarten, besides being a pleasant place for the normal child, can, I think, provide a valuable though only partial antidote to some of the bad effects of unwise home discipline such as we shall discuss in later chapters; and no doubt there is a special danger if the child who is kept home until five or six is an only child, or if there is no brother or sister of about the same age; but we have no proof that even so he cannot develop into a normal child if the parents beware of continuing to make a baby of him and otherwise treat him wisely.

The development of social impulses at two or three years

Some arguments in favour of little children of two or three mixing with others of similar age can, however, be advanced. There is general agreement among psychologists that for the satisfactory development of the child it is desirable that any dawning impulse or activity should have some outlet—though a precocious forcing may be bad: and some social impulses and feelings—affection, co-operation, and what is vaguely called sociability, do undoubtedly appear in little children to an appreciable extent before the ages of three or four. Active sympathy indeed may be shown before the age of two by children towards those they love. I have known, personally, children of this age to run to comfort mother or father when they have suffered some slight injury, and sympathy is shown towards animals at that age or shortly after. It may become extremely strong during the period of about three to four years.

As to sympathy towards other children, this also may appear at two, although it is more frequent at three or four. Many examples could be given even from the one small Birmingham Nursery School already referred to. For example, Tommy, aged 2, cried very much on first coming to school. His little brother, Bob, aged 4, when he heard the crying, first just cried sympathetically; then with an effort he recovered himself and began to comfort his little brother in a fatherly way, saying, 'It's all right, Tommy; Bobbie's here.'

In following the development of my own children, I was astonished to find that even at the early age of two and three, it was not necessary that the suffering should actually be seen for sympathy to be roused. Thus, one day, a boy (aged 2½) had been told by his mother of a little child who had no toys. Later on, he was heard crying gently in the nursery. The nurse went and asked why he was crying. He said he wanted to give some toys to the little boy who had none; and, later on, he insisted on giving me several of his toys for the little boy.[1] He did *not* grow up morbidly sympathetic!

As regards early sociability, several reliable observers stress the fact that individual differences are even greater than the age differences. Charlotte Bühler found that some children as early as 1½ begin to join in groups of three for play. There are embryonic 'gangs' of boys at 3;0.[2] Little Augustus, of the Nursery School mentioned above, certainly played in a gang and led it. Signs of leadership may appear at least by 4;0. I have known one girl of 6;0 who spontaneously took the part of assistant mistress at a school party, and who, my daughter said, would be more use in assisting evacuation than would some voluntary helpers she had known!

On the effect of early entry into the Nursery School some competent observers claim that to some extent earlier entry into the school hastened social development. The newcomer of 2 years at first takes little interest in others, but after a shy period he begins to respond to friendly advances, though at times he may 'hit out' and watch the effects.[3] He soon finds that the experiment does not pay. By about 3 he wants to play in pairs or groups of three or four. Quite commonly at 3;0 he 'comforts and helps others

---

[1] Here is a marked difference between the little child and the higher apes: for the famous psychologist Köhler noticed that his apes only showed sympathy with another suffering ape so long as they could see it suffering or hear its cry. Out of sight, it was out of mind. Unfortunately, some human beings seem to remain at the ape level.

[2] See article in *Handbook of Child Psychology*, p. 378.

[3] See K. Bridges, *Social and Emotional Development of the Pre-School Child*, p. 83.

in distress; and by 3 - 4 verbal criticism of one another's conduct begins'.

Of course, all is not peace in the group. Obstinacy and aggression appear also by 2 and 3, but these surely must be taken as normal developments. As we have seen, it may, perhaps, be regarded as a bad sign if a child, especially a boy, is 'too good' at the age of 2 and 3.

Excessive assertiveness or quarrelsomeness, however, will receive some checking from the rest of the children; and this may be one of the main values of early mixing with other children, especially when the only alternative is the society of a doting mother who gives way to every tantrum.

An interesting experiment was carried out on this very point of the training of one child by another of the same age.[1] Ten children, two years old, were put in pairs in a little playroom together for twenty minutes and watched by an invisible observer. They were provided with toys. The number of friendly and unfriendly acts of each child were counted. Within a period of a few weeks each child was paired with each of the others. Three main facts emerged:

(i) There were enormous differences. Child B performed 110 friendly acts and only 2 unfriendly acts; Child G performed 107 friendly acts and 3 unfriendly acts; whereas the least friendly child, C, performed 78 friendly acts and 56 unfriendly acts.

(ii) Even in this short time the proportion of friendly to unfriendly acts increased by about 50 per cent.

(iii) There was also a clear tendency for the most friendly children to receive the greatest number of unfriendly acts!

Even at this early age, then, little children begin to 'train'

---

[1] See I. G. Mengert, *Journal of Genetic Psychology*, Sept. 1931, Vol. 39, p. 393.

C

one another, though it does not follow that such training is always of a desirable kind.[1]

No proof that early schooling is essential for all

I have elaborated this general argument that most children by two or three have already those social impulses and interests which are the raw material of social training and of character, and that it is healthy for children at least after the age of two or three to mix freely with other children of the same age, because I am anxious to do full justice to what is probably the view of most child-psychologists. Nevertheless, I repeat that we have not as yet any proof that such early schooling is *essential* for the satisfactory training of all children, provided they have proper attention at home, and especially if they have brothers and sisters not much older or younger than themselves. The probable advantages of companionship of children of a similar age, however, do seem to make it advisable that an only child, or one without a brother or sister within a year or two of his own age, should be sent to a Nursery School or Kinder-garten soon after three years of age. If, however, this is not done in the case of a particular child it cannot be assumed that, should he develop into a 'difficult' child, this would have been avoided had he gone to school earlier.

[1] Detailed reports as to the early development of sympathy and social impulses will be found in the author's *Psychology of Early Childhood* (3rd edition, 1946) especially Chap. 16.

IV

THE TREATMENT OF PROBLEM. CHILDREN AND THE WORK OF THE CHILD GUIDANCE CLINIC

Uncertainty as to causes of cures at the clinics

We have seen reason to believe that the influence of the Nursery School may be invaluable for many children from two to five years old; and yet we cannot conclude that it is essential for all children.

The records of the Child Guidance Clinics also, I think, afford ample evidence of their value for specially difficult 'problem children'; but here again we must guard against some fallacious inferences which are being drawn from such successes, partly because the various methods of the clinics are likely to be, and to my knowledge have been, recommended for all 'difficult' children, even for those much less difficult than the children usually referred to the Clinics.

The chief of these fallacies is the assumption that the peculiar methods of a particular Clinic must be the main cause of the 'cures' or social readjustment of the 'problem' children. Now a summary of the results of 'follow-up' investigations in thirteen Child Guidance Clinics in America and England, covering nine hundred cases, shows that the proportion of cures is about the same in each of a group of clinics despite the differences in the types of treatment.[1] In two other Clinics also the results were about the same, though in one the treatment was psycho-analytic, and in the other hydrotherapeutic.[2]

[1] See 'The Later Social Adjustment of Problem Children', *Smith College Studies in Social Work*, VI, No. 1, 1935.

[2] Dr. R. D. Gillespie, who cites these cases, thinks that 'recovery' is often differently interpreted. See *Proceedings of the Child Guidance Inter-Clinic Conference*, 1937, p. 60.

The Director of another Clinic told me that some of the children on his waiting list were reported cured before it was possible to admit them: which reminds me of the saying of the famous French psychiatrist, Janet, that there are certain forms of nervous disease which will take their course and then disappear whatever is done. Happy, he adds, the physician into whose hands the patient falls when she is about to recover![1]

The improvement of some problem children merely through maturing has to be borne in mind when considering the claims of psycho-analytic treatment. Thus the treatment by psycho-analysis of one boy of 9;0 for stealing resulted in a cure—after eight months.[2] And some of Mrs. Klein's children were under treatment long enough to pay between 200 and 300 visits to her.

Dr. R. B. Cattell goes further, and states that when 'various objective investigations' have been made of the effects of treatment on psycho-analytic or Adlerian lines, 'It has sometimes been found that the recovery rates of the treated and untreated groups were regrettably similar.'[3]

Possible causes of improvement while at the clinic

As possible partial causes of the improvements under the influence of a clinic, I suggest the following influences: of those I have enumerated below one or more would be likely to provide a common element in the treatment of different Clinics and so account for some similarity of percentages. Some of them are also factors which can make the ordinary

[1] Dr. Max Mindé states that about one in three cases of Schizophrenia (or Dementia Praecox) in adolescence 'recovers spontaneously', either completely or enough for ordinary social life. See his book, *In Search of Happiness*, p. 135; he adds that in the majority of cases melancholia 'clears up entirely after some months', p. 185.

[2] See C. R. Rogers, *The Clinical Treatment of the Problem Child*, p. 334.

[3] *Proceedings of the Child Guidance Inter-clinic Conference*, 1937, p. 55.

school life an effective influence upon many difficult children from unfavourable homes.

(1) First, there is the effect of merely taking the child for part of his waking life out of the unfavourable environment of the home which has helped to cause his particular mental state or from the school where his bad attitude has become fixed. (Compare the results sometimes obtained merely by sending a difficult child to a good boarding school.) The experience of the Geneva Clinic led the authorities to the conclusion that if parents will not co-operate with the clinic, the undisciplined child must be taken away from the home.[1] Burt, as the result of his wide experience with London children, also concluded, as to aggressive children of violent temper, that, 'If the mother is a weak disciplinarian . . . it will be best to remove the child from her charge altogether.'[2] Though transference to the clinic does not remove the child from the mother entirely, it introduces a new source of control, lessens the predominant influence of the parents, and by persuasion may get them to alter their methods of discipline.

(2) Bringing the child into contact with new friendly people with whom he can start on a new level, and with a new type of approach, without the old antagonisms to parents or brothers and sisters which have become fixed (the same applies to a change of teacher). I suggest that usually, at each stage of increasing maturity, the child, by greater wisdom due to experience or to mere maturing, becomes capable of making new and better contacts with his fellows: though the old attitudes and habits of the earlier more irresponsible, less co-ordinated period, continue to-wards the individuals concerned with that earlier period, and especially towards the parents. Hence only new personal

---

[1] See *Les Enfants Difficiles* (p. 164), by M. Loosli-Usteri, Paris, 1935.
[2] *The Subnormal Mind* (2nd edition), p. 264.

contacts give a chance for improved social reactions to occur. Some of our play-therapists and child-analysts—like Margaret Lowenfeld and Susan Isaacs—may owe their successes much more to their personal charm and their happy manner with children than to their special methods or theories.

(3) In some cases some other event of importance has happened besides coming to the Clinic for treatment. For example, in one report we are told that one of the girls, who had been intensely jealous of her elder sister, improved shortly after her association with the Clinic; but it seems that, at the same time, she also obtained a job in which she was happy, and also acquired a boy friend who was approved by the mother! Is it surprising that jealousy of the elder sister was lessened, and that the relationship within the family was improved?

(4) There is yet another possible influence; the very fact that parents have finally decided to refer their child to a Child Guidance Clinic, or are brought up against the fact that the school thinks they should be so referred, means that they themselves are probably now in the frame of mind in which they believe that something serious must be done about it; and besides often co-operating with the Clinic and following its advice about discipline, etc., they tend to take steps (in addition to any suggested by the Clinic) which may be a partial cause of the improvement; just as when a patient, who takes some advertised medicine, and at the same time adopts various new health hints as to exercise, mastication, fruit eating, etc., which are recommended in the leaflet accompanying the medicine, may improve largely through these accompanying changes.

The removal to a new home

Since the above was written a report of the Birmingham Society in Aid of Nervous Children shows that even bad cases which the Clinic had failed to cure have been cured by removal to farms.[1] Possibly here the two main factors would be: (1) an improvement in physical health through living on the farm; (2) the complete removal from the home environment and perhaps from friends whose influence was bad.

The effect of removal to a foster home, when home conditions are unfavourable, is also amply shown in various reports summarized by Dr. Carl Rogers in *The Clinical Treatment of the Problem Child* (pp. 80–81). Roughly some 80 per cent to 90 per cent of mild cases were 'cured' by removal to foster homes and some 60 per cent of the more serious cases; he adds, however, that Dr. Healey found improvement in only 46 per cent of the children who were diagnosed as of 'abnormal mentality or peculiar personality' —nearly half of this type being of 'excessive stubbornness, bad temper', etc.

It would seem, then, that in many cases a 'problem' child may become satisfactorily 'adjusted' (to use current terms) through a change to a favourable environment, and without any special form of psychological treatment. This fact has a direct bearing on the next topic we consider.

Play-therapy[2]

A word must be said here about some recent ideas and practice in play-therapy as used in some of our Child Guidance Clinics and Psychological Institutes. One main idea is that undesirable behaviour in the child may be expressed in play-form and so eliminated. Some hold that

[1] See the *Report of the Birmingham Society in Aid of Nervous Children*, 1939.

[2] A fuller discussion of children's play will be found in the chapter on 'The Beginnings and Significance of Play,' in the author's *Psychology of Early Childhood*, 3rd edition, 1946.

the children must be told the real significance of their play: as one play-therapist put it to me, 'If a boy is aggressive towards his mother, and in the clinic hits a doll, he must be told that it is really his mother that he is hitting and wants to hit, and only then will it cure him.' The head of one of our leading clinics, however, while admitting that 'Sometimes the psychiatrist must interpret to the child the meaning of his play', adds: 'The value of this however seems to be doubtful and interpretation is often inadvisable and harmful.'[1]

The published evidence for such a specific curative value in certain types of symbolic play seems to me very flimsy. Improvements that do take place seem explicable by reasons we have already mentioned, and on the ground that any form of congenial play adds to the contentment and happiness and probably the health of the child and improves his relationship with those who provided such pleasant play for him.

If we examine the evidence of one of our leading exponents of play-therapy, Dr. Margaret Lowenfeld, we find, in accounts full of interest and very candid, that some of her child patients actually improved more rapidly when away from the Clinic on holiday![2] Furthermore, some of Dr. Lowenfeld's patients attended the clinic for the greater part of a year and the mere passage of time might account for improvement in some cases, for many normal children pass through difficult periods. The records of Dr. K. Bridges and other nursery school observers show this, and it is surely also a fact familiar to most teachers.[3] I myself noted such phases in at least three of my own children. Children who have improved

[1] Dr. Moodie in the *Report on the London Child Guidance Clinic for 1932–3*, p. 8. [2] See 'A New Approach to the Problem of Psycho-Neurosis in Childhood', *Brit. Jour. of Med. Psych*, XI, 1931, pp. 213, 215. [3] See articles by J. Cumming, referred to in Appendix, p. 103.

when undergoing play-therapy after the failure of other methods, may be improving because of this time-factor and maturation in a more congenial environment. (One of the mothers, for example, was described as temperamentally irritable with children and 'weepy'. Mere partial removal from her charge would probably be beneficial.)

Some of Dr. Lowenfeld's records indicate that *suggestion* also had some considerable influence, especially in those cases in which there was improvement when at the clinic but not when at home.[1]

Even if it were proved that in a few abnormal cases some play activities symbolize internal conflicts and could be the means of alleviating them, it does not follow that this would be true for the great majority of children—even the majority of those found somewhat difficult at home or in school. Yet there is a frequent tendency in semi-popular books on child psychology to slip almost imperceptibly from statements about problem children to the needs and treatment of more normal children, so that parents and teachers are apt to interpret the most innocent actions as profoundly significant of some present or future trouble unless special care be taken, and an attitude of excessive anxiety and fussiness may be aroused.[2] Furthermore, a reaction against child-psychology is to be feared if hypotheses which have been announced as dogmas are proved untenable, especially if it appears that familiarity with ordinary children should have made that clear all along.

---

[1] *Op. cit.*, p. 205 and p. 215.

[2] For example, a student with no previous training in the general psychology of childhood and little familiarity with young children, had a few weeks at a clinic in touch with a play-therapist. Shortly afterwards she visited a Nursery School, and seeing a child who was constantly climbing desks, tables, etc., said in a tone of deep emotional conviction, 'Ah, she feels her inferiority and so wants to raise herself in the world—to surmount difficulties!'

The need for research

The whole problem of the treatment of serious maladjustments of children is so complex that we need more centres in which the facts can be examined by critically-minded psychologists who are devotees of no particular school of thought.

Equally, if not more, desirable and important are 'follow-up' studies to see whether children who improved while at a Clinic are continuing satisfactorily at least several years later. Several Clinics have reported that it is so in a large percentage of cases. One extensive enquiry reveals more valuable details and also the possible dangers in interpreting the results of 'follow-up' enquiries. Miss H. L. Witmer and some collaborators obtained reports on nearly 200 children between $1\frac{1}{2}$ and $2\frac{1}{2}$ years after their treatment in the Institute for Child Guidance in New York.[1] It was found that, while the various percentages of successfully adjusted, partially adjusted, and unimproved was about the same after the $1\frac{1}{2}$ or $2\frac{1}{2}$ years, 'There was almost no relation between a patient's adjustment at the close of the case and his adjustment a few years later.' The changes, however, took place largely in the 'partially adjusted' groups: and of those previously marked A (successfully adjusted) on the five-point scale, very few were marked below C $1\frac{1}{2}$ years later: and of those marked D or E (unadjusted) very few had risen to A $1\frac{1}{2}$ or $2\frac{1}{2}$ years later.[2]

The following facts also brought out in this enquiry illustrate the influence of particular kinds of home conditions:

(1) Very few children from 'harmonious' homes were unimproved at the close of the treatment or later.

(2) Especially favourable too were homes where the

---

[1] See her article 'The Outcome of Treatment in a Child Guidance Clinic', in *Smith College Studies in Social Work*, June 1933, Vol. III, No. 4.
[2] *Op. cit.*, p. 397.

parents gave the children neither too much nor too little affection.

Lessons suggested for parents of a difficult child

These two facts, together with our earlier examination of the influence of the removal of a child to a Clinic, suggest that the main lessons of the experience of such Clinics for the intelligent parents of the difficult child are these:

(i) honestly to examine themselves and see that their own treatment of the child is not too severe or too indulgent;

(ii) to provide other society and other control besides their own, even additional to that given by a day-school;

(iii) to be willing in very serious cases if necessary to place the child in an entirely different environment. Of course, there must also be consideration of the health of the child, and as to whether defects in behaviour are due primarily to strong innate tendencies. It is here that the help of the expert psychologist will be most needed.

Most of the lessons gathered from the study of the Child Guidance Clinics have also a bearing on the problem of discipline, to which we must now turn.

Note.—Since this book was first printed there has appeared an interesting *Follow up Study of Child Guidance Patients*, by M. Shirley and others (Smith College Studies in Social Work, XI, p. 31, 1940). The subsequent careers of 85 children (of whom 50 had been 'cures' and 35 'failures') were studied at a period varying from 3 to 10 years after the time they were at the Clinic. It was found that eventually 40 % of the 'cures' at the Clinic had relapsed, and 40 % of the 'failures' had recuperated.

Part Two

THE PROBLEM OF DISCIPLINE

V

THE PROBLEM OF DISCIPLINE: (A) SOME
FADS AND FALLACIES

IN PART I of this book we have been discussing chiefly ideas which can be tested partly at least by a reference to facts. In this second part, in which we discuss discipline, while we shall refer to some facts of experience and occasionally to the records of investigations, we must recognize that we enter more debatable grounds. We may show that some dogmas are based on inadequate grounds: but we disclaim any wish to assert other rival dogmas. Often we can only appeal for a calm, unprejudiced judgment of what seems probable and reasonable. In this chapter we shall be concerned with the first type of problem—an examination of the bases of the doctrine of 'No repressive discipline'.

The revolt from Victorian severity

In Victorian days there seemed to be an excessive belief in discipline for its own sake, and a conviction that the sooner the child was turned into a little adult, by the repression of childish impulses and the imitation of adult self-restraint, the better it was for all concerned.

Few of us, I think, would wish for a return of the severity of those days. The revolt against it has been part of the general movement away from the harshness of punishment of wrongdoers, adult or juvenile, associated with an emphasis of the reformatory purpose of punishment rather than its vindictiveness. But as often happens, the reaction to an extreme form of thought or practice seems to have gone too far in some quarters. Some who felt there was something seriously wrong with Victorian discipline have uncritically accepted dogmatic assertions as to the evil results of all restraining discipline: and often the most confident pronouncements are made by persons who have brought up no children of their own, or have little or no experience of teaching.

The spreading of such views has been encouraged by the misunderstanding of the teaching of Montessori and other educational reformers; but in recent years they have been greatly accentuated by the doctrines of Freud and of Adler. Now, as I have already claimed, I have no prejudice against the teaching of Freud: and I would gladly join in the tributes so widely paid to Adler for having emphasized the great importance to the child of some satisfaction in his school life, some success which will prevent him from feeling a hopeless failure and developing an 'inferiority complex.'[1] What I would protest against is the over-emphasis of the supreme importance of *one* selected element in human nature—by Freud of the sex element and by Adler of self-assertion. Adler writes, for example, as though laziness were usually a cloak for concealing incapacity.[2] Sometimes it may be so: but here, as often, a wide generalization is not justified and may be dangerous.

Unfortunately it is much more likely to attract public attention if one selects one important aspect of mental life and makes sweeping statements about it. It sounds much more original. To say that there is a certain amount of truth in an idea, but that on the other hand there are certain objections to it, is dull and leaves us in a state of uncertainty. Say, like A. S. Neill, that *every* theft by a child is really an outcome of the craving for love, or that most of a boy's

[1] This paragraph and parts of the next two pages are quoted by courtesy of the editor from an article of mine 'Discipline and the Psychology of the Unconscious', published in *The New Schoolmaster*, 1937.
[2] See his *Education of Children* (George Allen and Unwin).

mental troubles are due to his thinking masturbation is wrong, and your lectures, as he says of his own, are 'crowded out'.[1] So many people like to be stimulated by novel ideas and dislike suspending judgment. They dislike also acting upon mere probabilities; unfortunately, that is what we must be content to do to a large extent at present if we are to maintain a scientific attitude towards psychological problems of discipline.

Repression: its meaning and effects

In considering the work of Freud one must bear in mind two things especially: first, that he began as a medical man and was later a specialist in nervous diseases. Thus, his 'material' has hardly been typical; yet he built up a theory of human nature largely on evidence gained from neurotics. Secondly, when the dangers of repression are discussed one has to bear in mind that Freud is concerned chiefly with repression of the powerful impulse of sex. Even here, in statements apt to be ignored by the enthusiast, he is cautious enough himself to say that licence is not a solution of the problem and that any harm due to repression depends partly upon the strength of the nervous system of the individual concerned. Thus, he leaves a loophole for the view that harm from repression may only accrue to a minority of individuals. Thirdly, by 'repression' is really meant, not what the plain man usually thinks, but blindly shirking the issue instead of facing it squarely and consciously choosing one of the two alternatives, with a frank recognition of the sacrifice involved, or reconciling the two in a higher synthesis. But, having got hold of this idea that 'repression is harmful' some people unwittingly transfer the word to the repression of every kind of impulse; so that it may be held that it is harmful to make a child repress an impulse to throw a stone

[1] See his recent book *That Dreadful School*, pp. 160 and 166.

D

through a window, or to punch a little playmate's head, or even the impulse to drum with his fingers on the desk during a lesson, or other impulses scarcely of profound biological importance. It is indeed astonishing to find some educated people so quickly develop the view that all firm discipline of children is wrong.

Lax discipline

Many examples have come within the experience of the writer or of intimate friends with psychological training. In some cases serious misdemeanours bring only a mild and even laughing reproof. On one occasion I was playing tennis with friends on their own court: their boy of about 9 years kept running across the court and spoiling the game. When he finally ran behind me and administered a hard smack on my back with a tennis racket, all that happened was that the mother said, 'Isn't it a pity'?—as though the boy's behaviour was an act of God and nothing could be done about it!

One of my sons, who is a doctor, reported to me the following case. A little girl of 4;0 was allowed by her indulgent mother to become completely dominant. Her continued tantrums, etc., accentuated a nervous collapse of the mother (her doctor thought they actually caused it), so that the child had to be sent away to the grandparents. Here firmness combined with kindness was exercised, and within a few weeks the little girl's behaviour was completely changed.

Sometimes the parents foolishly reveal to the child himself their own impotence. Once when I was with my boy of 9 years in an hotel, a lady expressed astonishment that I could go out to the theatre and trust my boy to go to bed of his own accord at nine o'clock. The mother continued, 'When I tell Mary (a girl of similar age who was then present, though it was very late) to go to bed, she won't go': and the mother smiled at Mary with a fond, fatuous expression.

These are examples of types of discipline which have regrettable consequences to both parents and children. Indeed, some children themselves may come to regret such laxity. For, as Dr. Cyril Norwood said in his admirable book, *The English Tradition of Education*, 'Boys are strange creatures who play the fool and yet strongly resent the fact that they are allowed to do it.' One of my own boys, when a young man, told me I ought to have 'coshed' him more![1] Some children themselves seem to have more sense here than the advocates of extreme freedom. I told two of my own children some time ago about a certain experimental school in which children were allowed to do pretty much as they liked, and gave a few examples of what is permitted. My boy of 13 listened quietly and then said, 'Is this a new kind of religion, or are the people dotty?'

Certainly, if adults do not put any restraint upon the more selfish or violent actions of aggressive children, other children are likely to do so, sometimes with less moderation. I have known either among my own acquaintances, or as the result of being consulted about some difficult child, a number of families in which both parents (or the dominant parent) have held the view that any firm discipline was wrong, or have been unwilling to undertake it, and in which the child became ill-mannered, inconsiderate and even tyrannical. As I was revising this book for publication I

[1] Apart from restraint through penalties, the decisions of one in authority seem to be welcomed at times, as saving conflict and avoiding a responsibility which the child feels unable to take. I have occasionally known a boy, who was usually self-confident and normally assertive, beg me to make a decision for him as to what he ought to do. We may recall the statement of Pierre Janet that by the decisions of one in authority the neurotic patient may be 'rid of . . . higher operations that demand great expenditure' of energy. (*Principles of Psycho-Therapy*, p. 205).

heard two officers and a friend each deploring the spoiling of children in different families known to them, by these ideas of easy discipline and no punishment. One told us of a girl of 8;0 who was never restrained by the mother; one day this headstrong child took a glowing cinder in the tongs and placed it on the back of a dog belonging to one of the officers. The animal's howls of pain roused his master to firm handling of the child, for which he was severely taken to task by the mother. One of my advanced students, an experienced teacher, writes that 'teachers are often implored by parents to extend indulgence towards anti-social behaviour of all types lest the child should grow up "repressed" '.

I must remind myself of the dangers of judging from a limited number of cases; but if we turn again to Burt's enquiry on juvenile delinquency, we read that while over-strictness was found in only 10 per cent of his cases, too weak and easy-going discipline was found in 25 per cent of his cases.[1] On the other hand, among Burt's Control Group of 200 non-delinquent children living in similar houses in the same streets, weak discipline of a similar degree was rarely found, scarcely more often indeed than over-strict discipline.[2] Lax discipline and over-petting, by the mother especially, also often occur in reports on home conditions of 'problem' children as we shall see later; and there is general agreement that the absence of fathers on war service, and the usually easier discipline of the mothers, have a bad effect on the development of some children.

[1] *The Young Delinquent*, p. 97. Defective discipline of some kind gave a much higher correlation with crime (viz. 0·55) than did poverty (0·15) or defective family relations (0·33) and even higher than vicious homes (0·39). *Op. cit.*, p. 101. Further facts will be given in a later chapter in the discussion of punishment. Elsewhere Burt, whose experience in dealing with difficult and neurotic children is a wide one, writes: 'Never should a child be allowed to grow up knowing that he can gain his ends by a wild emotional display.' (*The Subnormal Mind*, p. 264.)

[2] *Op. cit.*, Table on pp. 64–65.

There seems, then, to be a real danger of an excessive laxity of discipline, encouraged as it has been by vague ideas of the harmfulness of repression. It is, I think, very probable that the frequent appearance of 'problem' children in 'broken' homes, is partly due to the fact that in such homes the discipline is likely to be inadequate, inconsistent, and erratic, and especially too lax; either because there is only a mother in the home, or, if there is only a father, because he is unable to exercise proper supervision through being out most of the day.

At other times, no doubt, excessively severe discipline or too constant supervision and dominance seem to be causes of trouble. Though nowadays this is not so frequent, we shall have to bear it in mind later on.

We may safely conclude that we have ample reason for considering in fuller detail this problem of discipline.

Discipline not identical with punishment

Before closing this chapter, however, we must ward off two possible misunderstandings, the first as to the meaning of this term 'discipline'. It is far from being identical with punishment and still further from corporal punishment. Though penalties may be necessary at times, both parent and teacher can 'keep good discipline' with very little, or even no punishment so far as the majority of children are concerned. Some helps to such a restraining influence we shall discuss in later chapters in which it is hoped the essentials of 'good discipline' will become clearer.

The need for legitimate freedom

Second, while I have argued that there are no psychological grounds for the doctrine that all punishment and restraint are wrong, I should hold equally strongly that it is far better to secure the desirable results so far as possible by praise and encouragement, and also (so far as is consistent with the child's physical health, moderate educational progress and respect for the rights of others), he should be given as much freedom as possible. In infancy I suggest that he should have if possible at least part of an attic and part of a garden where he can make as much noise and as big a mess as he likes, provided he does his share of clearing up; in middle childhood he should have substantially the choice of how he spends his leisure time at home, with of course a parental veto on late nights, unsuitable or too many 'pictures', etc.; and though some healthy exercise in the open air should be insisted on there should be no compulsory games if he hates them, and no prohibition of 'penny dreadfuls' if he loves them—though I should try to provide tempting alternatives. In the big things, too, freedom should I think be given. Religious parents make a mistake I think in *forcing* church-going on their children. When our own children were very young, visits to church were a privilege and usually withheld till the children could understand a little and control undue fidgetiness; it was never compulsory. Later, the choice of a profession should ultimately be left to the youth himself, all the pros and cons being put before him. The parents may, of course, have to veto certain choices as being beyond their means: and if the choice has to be made as early as 14 years, no doubt it may be better for parents in consultation with the Juvenile Employment Bureau or some vocational guidance agency to make the final decision.

The question of the choice of the profession has taken us away from matters of direct discipline; but it comes under general parental *control*, and I mention it to illustrate how much freedom for the youth I would personally advocate. The question of freedom will be discussed further in the next chapter.

VI

THE PROBLEM OF DISCIPLINE: (B) REPRESSION, SUBLIMATION AND THE INFERIORITY COMPLEX

Repressive discipline not enough

While the psychology of repression gives no adequate ground for abandoning firm discipline, including, if necessary, punishment, we may nevertheless learn much of real value from the new psychology of the unconscious. For while discipline and restraint are necessary for the child's own present health and future welfare, as well as for the reasonable quietness and efficient working of home and school, there is no virtue in discipline for its own sake; yet the idea that there is, is still active in some homes and schools. For example, some of my teacher-students assure me that the custom still exists in some classes of making pupils sit with arms folded in perfect silence for a few minutes; and the rule in some girls' schools of forbidding the pupils to converse in corridors even when there is a general break, seems to me equally unnecessary and foolish.

Again, in view of the fact that repression of an impulse seems often to result in its breaking out in another form, 'sublimation' where possible is better than repression. By sublimation is meant the raising of an impulse to a higher level, the provision for the impulse of an outlet which has a better social value than the natural or primitive one. It is believed by many, for example, that in providing boys with competitive games, such as football, we are giving an opportunity to the players to employ their pugnacious impulses in a harmless way. There is usually the further belief that as a result they are likely to be less pugnacious or aggressive in everyday life; that this play will have a

cathartic effect. Personally I cannot see that this latter is
proved; though some general psychological arguments, particularly evidence based on a study of the unconscious,
make it seem probable that sublimation does in some cases
take place in the full sense, namely that the impulse is
actually turned away from the natural object.[1] The elderly
spinster does seem to find satisfaction for the maternal
instinct in the devotion to a pet dog, though here we should
speak of 'displacement' rather than sublimation. Perhaps
one of the best examples of sublimation is the story of the
way in which the founder of the George Junior Republic
deflected the gang of young 'toughs', in whom he took an
interest, from fighting against the police as they formerly
had, to fighting on the side of the law.[2]

Certainly, the possibility of sublimation seems sufficiently
great to justify this general rule: that in the home, and in
free play periods in school, the natural impulses of the
child should be given freedom and opportunity for expression, so far as this is consistent with their own welfare and
with equal freedom for others. As regards school work,
legitimate self-assertion and self-respect must not be perpetually thwarted by work which is beyond the child's
powers, or by a domination in school (or home) which
leaves no scope for self-direction.

[1] I have discussed the nature of sublimation and the evidence for it
more fully in my little book *The New Psychology of the Unconscious*,
Chap. 8. There is an illuminating discussion of 'Repression and Sub-
limation' in Chap. 16 of Godfrey Thomson's *Instinct, Intelligence and
Character*; and an extremely clear treatment of the subject in R. H.
Thouless's *General and Social Psychology*, Chap. 8. An article by J Flügel
on 'Freudian Mechanisms as Factors in Moral Development' (*British
Journal of Psychology*, Vol. VIII), though published as long ago as 1917,
remains, in my opinion, one of the ablest expositions of the orthodox
Freudian view on this topic, with many clarifying suggestions made by
Flügel himself.

[2] *Citizens Made and Remade*, by W. A. George and L. B. Stone.

For impulses which themselves might take a harmful direction as, for example, the love of adventure, we should seek to provide or suggest harmless channels. *One should never be content with merely repressive discipline.*

This seems to be in general a sound principle on which to work. Yet I would suggest that when self-assertiveness is very strong and combined with lack of sympathy or affection for others, opportunities for successful self-assertion may actually strengthen the bad habits. Some tyrants we know seem to feed on success and grow greater bullies. It is true that some troublesome, restless, assertive children seem to be improved, or at least palliated, by the chances of self-display afforded by acting or by the importance of being a monitor; but others seem to be made more 'cocky'—more self-satisfied and assertive. I have noticed similar differences of effects in adults as the results of wider recognition or of the acquisition of greater power.

I would suggest that the beneficial results in such cases occur when there is a genuine inferiority complex, or a conscious awareness of a lack of just appreciation of one's work; while harmful results are more likely to follow when the cause of the trouble is really an exceptionally strong innate assertiveness not balanced by more social impulses.

It is often no doubt very difficult to detect with certainty to which of these types a child belongs; we can only study the individual's reactions and watch the effects of our efforts, not expecting too rapid a change.

Sublimation and substitution

We must mention here a sense in which the word sublimation is incorrectly used. Sometimes it is thus applied when a child is encouraged to take up an entirely different kind of activity from the one which he is naturally apt to follow. For example, it may be urged, quite rightly, that

youths are less likely to wander about the streets and perhaps get into the hand of the law by stealing or trespassing
if they are provided with a club-room in which they can
play billiards or chess.[1] Yet it can hardly be suggested that
in stealing and in chess precisely the same impulses and
activities are involved.[2] It is rather an application of the
old adage, 'Satan finds some mischief still for idle hands to
do', the truth of which was amply shown again by the
many pranks and misdemeanours of children when their
schools were closed in the early months of the present war.

To this commonplace idea that everything which will
keep a child occupied makes it less likely that he will get
into mischief, the modern psychology of the unconscious
has added a new point, namely, that so far as possible we
should seek to use the *same* 'impulse', which has been used
in a mischievous way, in some other and better activity,
and not merely to get the child to substitute *another* impulse
for the mischievous one. Nevertheless, even granted that
this may be desirable when possible, we should bear in

[1] Evidence of the relation between juvenile delinquency and lack of
membership of any club or social organization is given by W. L. Chinn
in an aticle in the *British Journal of Educational Psychology*, Vol. VIII,
1938. Mr. Chinn studied the cases of nearly one thousand young delinquents in Birmingham.

[2] No doubt there may be some elements in common: for example,
the satisfaction of the self-assertive or competitive impulse which enters
into the enjoyment of victory in chess may also enter as an element
when a boy prides himself on having brought off a clever theft. In some
cases indeed this may be the principle element. But it seems to me to
show a lack of a sense of proportion to stress this against the evident
advantages gained in most cases through the money or goods stolen.
In a few abnormal cases, it is true, the goods stolen are of trivial value
and the repetition of the stealings of the same unwanted article may be
explained by some outstanding emotional experience; e.g. Healey attributes one youth's strange habit of stealing only horses and traps to the
fact that a man was driving the youth in a trap when he introduced
him first to some of the mysteries of sex. (See W. Healey, *Mental Conflicts and Misconduct*, p. 108, London, 1920.)

mind the great element of truth in the old adage just quoted. For we cannot regard the actions of children or adults as simply issuing from their own impulses independently of external influences, but rather as the result of the response of these inner tendencies to the world around them. Now it is quite true that an impulse may be so strong that it may urge a man to go out as it were to seek the appropriate stimulus; but some of the impulses are not of this kind, especially in childhood; they do not necessarily require satisfaction. They may arise if the appropriate stimulus appears, or to put it in more popular words, if the temptation is put before them and if there is no equally attractive alternative; but if the children are occupied in doing other things the temptations are less likely to occur and less likely to appeal when they do occur. I remember hearing Cecil Chesterton in a speech on the reform of Public Houses claim that there would be less drunkenness in the public houses if music or other kinds of entertainment were provided. As things were, he argued, a man would drink more and more through 'sheer fidgetiness'!

Self-assertion and the inferiority complex

There is one great propensity which is of special importance during the period of childhood, and is apt to dominate much of his life long before the impulse of sex is active; that is the impulse of self-assertion. Neither child nor adult likes to feel himself greatly inferior to others. It grieves us to have all our activities thwarted by others, to be dominated by others, except perhaps by a few for whom we feel great admiration or affection, with whom it may be a joy to be submissive and to accept their will as law. These impulses of self-assertion and self-submission vary greatly in their strength in different individuals. In some children one is much stronger than the other. In a few self-submission seems predominant. In most, however, the impulse of self-assertion seems much stronger and more constantly in evidence. Indeed, as we have seen, it has been suggested that the absence of any sign of strong self-assertion before the age of 3 or 4, is a sign of some deficiency in the child.

The prominence of this impulse of self-assertion led Adler to centre his theory of human personality around it, and to connect it in some way with practically all problems of discipline in childhood. The child's 'chief purpose', he wrote, is 'to dominate those who are gathered about him.'[1] Dr. Adler's keen sympathy with children and his fine enthusiasm for the better handling of children unfortunately led him to exaggerate the importance of this impulse, and of the 'inferiority complex' which may develop if the impulse of self-assertion is thwarted too much. As with Freud's explanation of sex in childhood, there is a lack of proportion in Adler's stressing of self-assertion.[2]

Laziness or stupidity?

This lack of proportion is also shown, I think, when Adler writes as though laziness were usually a cloak for a stupidity of which the child is aware. No doubt it is sometimes: for usually as Adler says, 'It is less painful to be told one is lazy than that one is incapable.'[3] But to some children it may be less painful to be thought incapable than it is to work hard at an uncongenial task; and lack of interest is not identical with lack of capacity though no doubt the two are closely related. It is sometimes said that for pupils to be labelled as belonging to a 'C' class is disheartening and

[1] *Understanding Human Nature*, p. 34 (London, 1927).
[2] There is also at times a lack of a sense of humour, perhaps closely allied. Thus Adler wrote: 'A boy, asked what he wanted to be in later life, said, "I want to be a hangman." 'This', commented Adler, 'displays a lack of social interest'! (*The Science of Living*, p. 55, London, 1929).
[3] See *The Education of Children*, p. 66.

harmful; and that I should imagine is true of most. One of my teacher-students, however, relates that in his Senior School he has known the 'C' class pupils to say to a teacher: 'Please Sir, we are only "C" pupils, you can't expect us to do so much or so well as the others.' (Perhaps they were not so 'C' as they were labelled!) In a large group of elementary school teachers, most were amused at the idea that 'C' children are worried about their being labelled 'C'; but of course the teacher does not always know the child's inner feelings: and whether laziness is usually a pose or not, it may sometimes be, and the possibility should make us wary.[1]

There certainly seems no justification for ever telling a child he is stupid. Records I have had from my students show that the sharp tongue of a teacher may depress and even embitter a pupil for years. Some students indeed attribute their permanent dislike of a subject to their having studied it under a teacher who was too critical or antagonistic. (In one class of graduate students in training, 10 out of 48 men and 12 out of 44 women declared that this was their own experience; but no doubt other factors helped towards this dislike.)

As to labelling pupils 'C', it would be better as far as possible to base the selection of the 'C' groups on the possession of some ability other than those shown especially by the 'A' group, for example ability for craft work. In some schools they are called the 'Practical' classes.

The need for work in which success is possible

One other practical inference seems justifiable. Even the dull child should have some kind of work provided in which

---

[1] The cause of 'laziness' seems in fact to be of various kinds. It may be physical, due to general ill-health, or due to an apathetic temperament, or to neurasthenia and excessive fatiguability, or to too difficult or unsuitable work; the last of these causes we discuss in the next section.

he can make good progress which he himself can recognize. In the early days when handwork was first being introduced into the elementary schools, competent observers came to the conclusion that it improved the general attitude towards school of many of the pupils. In some schools a decided drop in the frequency of corporal punishment coincided with the introduction of handwork.[1]

The highly academic curriculum for Matriculation, imposed as it was until recently on nearly all pupils in secondary schools, led to disheartenment in many. A very able and experienced headmaster once said to me that it was a pathetic sight to see so many of his pupils, at first keen and happy, gradually acquiring an 'inferiority complex' in a hopeless struggle with work too difficult for them. In an enquiry by one of my research students among secondary school pupils as to which subjects they liked or disliked and why, typical replies in reference to Latin (which came bottom on the list among 3,000 boys, being ousted from that position among the girls only by geometry) referred to the hopelessness of progress: 'I cannot understand it however hard I try'; 'I can't get it clear though I have tried very hard'; 'I dread the lesson coming'; 'All my efforts seem in vain'; 'I often spend an hour instead of half an hour on my Latin homework, and get more punishment for it than for any other work.'[2]

One girl, whom I knew intimately and who had excellent

---

[1] See Dr. P. B. Ballard's *Handwork as an Educational Medium*, 2nd edition, especially pp. 104 and 105. C. R. Rogers states that 'problem children tend to show better ability than the average in manual tests along with a below-average showing in tests of abstract intelligence' (*The Clinical Treatment of the Problem Child*, p. 231). The evidence is summarized on p. 136.

[2] For full details of this enquiry see R. A. Pritchard's article in *The British Journal of Educational Psychology*, Vol. V, 1935. I have given a fuller account of the results about Latin in my book, *Latin: Its Place and Value in Education*, Chap. I (London University Press, 1935).

ability for languages and literature, felt hopeless about her mathematics, and for a time it cast a gloom over her school life. Her whole attitude to school was altered when she was allowed to drop mathematics; and several of my women students have reported similar experiences. Sometimes an unsuspected specific weakness of a very serious kind (e.g. specific reading disability) prevents progress in nearly all subjects, and results in a hopeless feeling of failure in a child of good general intelligence. Many examples of such disabilities are given by Cyril Burt in his book, *The Backward Child*. A close relation between 'problem tendencies' and failure in school achievement was found by W. C. Olsen, the correlation being about 0·57 among 63 fifth-grade children.[1]

Though understanding as to the importance of specific abilities is much wider than it was, the idea that pupils can always 'do a subject if they try hard enough' is by no means dead; and where there is genuine but fruitless effort to succeed, there is likely to be either open revolt or the growth of a hopeless feeling of incompetence, which may or may not develop into an 'inferiority complex'.

The meaning and causes of the inferiority complex

The proper meaning of this term and the significance of the complex if it develops, we must consider for a moment. Much of the popular talk and semi-popular writing about the inferiority complex is vague and ill-balanced. It sometimes ignores the facts of innate individual differences which were stressed in Chapter II. Some children have a relatively weak impulse of self-assertion, and a strong tendency to self-submission: in popular language they are 'modest' and 'yielding'. They frankly admit their limitations and may be extremely diffident.

[1] See his *Problem Tendencies in Children*, p. 53 (Minneapolis, 1930).

All this, however, does not constitute a 'complex'; for a complex implies some impulse or idea and attendant feelings which are *repressed*, at least partially, but reveal themselves in another form, including irrational or exaggerated actions. A more probable sufferer from a genuine inferiority complex is the person who, once realizing his inferiority in some respects, cannot tolerate the feeling, represses it and unconsciously compensates for it by blustering, boasting manners, conspicuous dress, etc., or possibly, in extreme cases, by securing attention and satisfaction through rebellion and even minor criminal acts. There is a sense, of course, in which all children feel inferior to the powerful and experienced adult: but this again is not the same as an inferiority complex.

The conditions for the development of an inferiority complex seem to be as follows:

(1) a strong self-assertive impulse or a 'proud spirit';
(2) deficiency in abilities or qualities which would bring satisfaction in social life.

When the deficiency is very obvious, as in some serious physical disability, the fact of course cannot be ignored; but if assertiveness is very strong, there is likely, I think, to result violent and exaggerated counter-actions, the *connection* of which with the physical weakness is not realized or is actually repressed. (Whether this should be labelled a complex we need not here discuss.) The partially paralysed arm of the former Kaiser Wilhelm may well have been a factor in accentuating his boasting and assertiveness; his own autobiography indeed (*The Story of My Early Life*) shows that he was very sensitive about this defect. The physical deficiencies of the poet Pope have been suggested as partial causes of his bitter irony in dealing with some of his contemporaries; and Byron's deformed foot, and his mother's cruel jibe, 'lame brat', no doubt had their effects.[1]

Though a physical defect may be fully realized by a child he is likely to be quite unaware of the fact that his blustering is partly dependent on this feeling of deficiency. There is 'dissociation' even if there is not absolute repression.[2]

Another conceivable cause of trouble is the lack of love in childhood. Adler indeed attributes to this the hardness and hatred of all tyrants. Exact statistical support is lacking, but the records of Child Guidance Clinics reveal the frequency with which the unloved child is found among the 'problem children',[3] and on general grounds it seems likely that a child who feels he is unloved by one or both parents, will become envious and jealous, will tend to act in a way to attract attention or to assert himself, and may, in accordance with the tendency well known to psycho-therapeutists, develop some minor illness that secures sympathy. It seems likely that if he is to be freed from any such complex a child would need the provision of some affection of which he has been starved; and such provision may be one of the causes of the improvement in some children in the friendly

[1] See *Parents and Children: an Anthology*, by Hugh Kingsmill, p. 105 (The Cresset Press, London, 1936).

[2] I have suggested elsewhere that dissociation rather than complete repression is characteristic of more normal persons. See *The New Psychology of the Unconscious*, p. 153 ff. (2nd edition, Christophers, 1928).

[3] That lack of affection in both parents is the worst parent relationship for problem children, and that the problem child who is unloved by the mother (especially) is also particularly hard to cure, are suggested by the report by Helen Witmer and students, *Smith College Studies in Social Work*, Vol. III, No. 4 (1933), p. 370. But the numbers were very small and the results for the children who were *over*-protected by the mother and for those who were an outlet for her emotions, were about the same.

E

atmosphere of the school or Child Guidance Clinic or of some foster homes.[1]

Of course the showing of such affection to neglected and rebellious children is not inconsistent with firmness in checking their misdeeds, and should I think be accompanied by such discipline; but when any wrong has been penalized, and any loss by other children compensated for, friendly relations with the offender should be attempted again.

To return to those suffering from some physical defect or mental disability; here the difficulty is to strike the happy medium between excessive sympathy or over-petting on the one hand, and neglect or hardness on the other. In some cases a physical weakness can be used by an assertive child to obtain a tyrannical hold on an over-anxious mother. Whether the child is of this or the opposite type, gentler and depressed through his disability, we must seek to give him chances of success in ways other than those from which he is debarred. The lame child may become a good craftsman or artist, or read more widely than his fellows. Justice demands that he should have certain special privileges because of his disability, that he should ride when others walk, and have some extra entertainment for lack of active games, but hardly that he should in everything take precedence of his brothers and sisters. As he grows older it may be possible to indicate to him a few compensations for his defects; and at least for him to be led to see that the best of his acquaintances will not look down on him for a bodily defect, as they would dislike him for selfishness or aggressiveness.

[1] How quickly very young children may respond to affectionate treatment has been exemplified in some of the Nursery or Infant School children who have been evacuated. Even though the majority of mothers are no doubt loving and devoted, many of the youngsters, as I myself have seen, rapidly become happy and contented though separated from their parents if they have the right kind of treatment in their new surroundings.

The 'nervous' child

Children suffering from the personal defects just referred to, or unhappy through lack of love at home or failure in school work, may appear depressed and fearsome and sometimes would be called in popular language 'nervous'. Apart from this particular difficulty of the inferiority complex, and some later discussion of the adaptations of discipline to the diffident, submissive child, I do not propose to discuss the 'nervous' child; partly because, as indicated in the opening pages, this book is mainly concerned with the 'naughty', obstinate or aggressive child and the problems of his discipline; and partly because the so-called 'nervous' child so often suffers from some innate physiological defect which requires the treatment of the medical man. But we shall see that discipline and especially punishment need careful adjustment to the case of the diffident, nervous, submissive child.[1]

[1] On the nervous child and those who seem diffident, apathetic, lacking in energy, etc., see the section headed 'The sensitive and repressed' in Sir Cyril Burt's comprehensive work *The Backward Child* (pp. 546 ff.), and also the chapter on 'Asthenic Neuroses' in his book *The Subnormal Mind*.

VII

SOME PRINCIPLES OF SOUND DISCIPLINE

IN CHAPTER V an attempt was made to combat the motion that all restraining discipline is wrong or harmful. In the last chapter it was agreed that though repressive, or better, preventive, discipline may be necessary at times, it should be replaced as far as possible by the sublimation of ill-directed impulses, or at least by the encouragement of other less harmful activities.

Stress has also been laid upon the need *to seek out and deal with the main causes of trouble*, the desirability of making it 'easy to be good' at least in early childhood, and of providing for activities appropriate to the age and interests of the child. This we may regard as the first principle of sound discipline.

Self-control—the aim of discipline

This general position is closely allied to a second guiding principle that *all discipline should aim at development of self-control*: with the corollary that as far as possible the child should be led to see the reason and justification for any discipline. Such explanation should follow more and more as his capacity to understand develops. This principle that all discipline should aim at eventual self-control would be admitted both by those who believe in entire freedom for children and by those who believe that discipline, and at times even severe punishment, may be necessary. So we need hardly discuss it further except to point out that some merely *preventive* discipline may at times be needed (1) for the health and safety of the child; (2) to prevent annoyance to others; (3) occasionally to prevent the wasting of time and to compel the early stages of study, or other work, which may later open up opportunities of intellectual enjoyment. This last no doubt is liable to great abuse, but so is the opposite idea that at every moment the child's immediate interest must be the sole guide of what he does. Such disciplinary pressure may be justified at some stages to carry the child over dull patches of work, but only if this will bring him eventually to success and enjoyment which he himself can then realize makes the earlier compulsory efforts worth while.[1]

I propose now to discuss briefly the application of several other general principles which seem to me sound, and to discuss some more doubtful problems of rewards and punishments, including corporal punishment. To a considerable extent these other principles are important as adjuncts to securing the last-mentioned aim, namely, that discipline should lead to self-control.

The principle of gradualness

Our third principle is that the *standard of conduct expected should not rise too suddenly*. It is obvious that we cannot expect from a three-year-old what we can reasonably expect from a ten-year-old. True, in certain matters we may expect more explicit obedience from the younger child to commands the reason for which he cannot appreciate; but in the earlier years we must not demand much in the way of general self-control; we must not expect a little child suddenly to break off a bad habit without relapses.

It must be admitted that this principle of the gradual raising of the standard of conduct does not give very definite guidance: for the parent may have little or no experience

---

[1] This last point is dealt with in the chapter on 'The doctrine of "grind", and the training of attention' in my book on *Latin: Its Place and Value in Education.*

of other children as a guide to what is normal; and in any case children vary so much in temperament and disposition, that some do naturally those things which others do only after long and careful training. We must also at times consider what allowance we must make for such things as temporary ill-health, or for the fact that a little child has 'worked itself up' into a state of anger or a fit of crying so that it cannot immediately check itself whoever appeals to it or whatever the threats of punishment or promises of reward may be.

When a child is at school a parent may check the standard of conduct he requires of the child, by school reports. The spoilt mother's darling at home is apt to have more severe criticism of his behaviour at school: while the parent who is strongly dissatisfied with a child who invariably gains good reports on his conduct at school, should consider whether he is not asking too much of the child. The check is not infallible, however, for lack of ability may be interpreted at school as laziness, at least for a time; or a cunning child may soon find he will suffer if he does not conform to standard at school and yet may continue to take advantage of weakness at home.

As to younger children, some guidance as to usual standards of conduct may be obtained from published psychological studies of normal young children, showing what is usual at various ages. Thus, on the basis of her studies of children in a Nursery School, Dr. K. M. Bridges gives certain generalizations as to social conduct characteristic of various ages; for example, that children over $3\frac{1}{2}$ years are 'often willing to share their possessions brought from home while those younger usually cling to them jealously', and that children of 3 or 4 years will quite commonly taunt others with their shortcomings though they will at times try to comfort another child in distress.[1]

---

[1] *Social and Emotional Development of the Pre-School Child*, p. 84.

The study of early childhood makes one fact abundantly clear, namely, that the parents must not expect that the little child will always refrain from serious lapses from what seems to an adult desirable conduct. Thus nearly every child shows great obstinacy at some period and also fits of anger, which have been found especially prevalent about the age of two in one group of children observed.[1] I have already given examples (in Chapter I) of occasional serious trouble in early years with children whose conduct on the whole was very satisfactory and who developed well later. Judging by recent figures even masturbation is to be expected in a small number of little children and in a considerable proportion of adolescents.[2]

Another general fact clearly established is that in all these respects there are great individual differences: and apart from that, each child fluctuates in his progress. We must expect occasional lapses, and be content if we find on the whole some improvement in social adjustment from year to year.

To give full information here on typical behaviour at various stages would mean the expansion of this book into a large volume on the psychology of childhood and adolescence; those who wish to go more fully into the matter must be referred to special books on the different periods.[3]

---

[1] See E. Goodenough, *Anger in Young Children.*

[2] See Leo Kanner, *Child Psychiatry*, p. 399 (London, 1936) and Charlotte Bühler, *From Birth to Maturity*, p. 64 and p. 182 (London, 1935).

[3] For the period of 2;0 to 5;0 see Dr. K. M. Bridge's book already referred to; Chap. IV in Ch. Bühler's *From Birth to Maturity*; C. W. Valentine's *Psychology of Early Childhood*, and A. Gesell *The First Five Years of Life.* The behaviour of somewhat older children in an experimental school in which great freedom was allowed is described by S. Isaacs in her *Social Development in Young Children*; but such a school is apt to attract children who are not quite an average sample. Much material on later periods will be found in the encyclopaedic *Handbook of Child Psychology* (edited by Carl Murchison), especially the chapters on Emo-

Although the guidance from this principle can only be vague and general, the parent or teacher can at least bear it in mind and try by comparative observations or enquiry to see whether he is setting much too high or too low a standard for his own charges compared with what is done by others.

One thing can at least be definitely avoided, namely, the putting too big a strain on the child's capacity to withstand temptation of various kinds, before a habit is well established. I heard recently of a little girl of $5\frac{1}{2}$ years who was found stealing some of the eleven o'clock luncheon of other children in the infant class. It was discovered that this child never brought any lunch: yet she had to sit with the others as they eat and even join in saying grace! This is precisely the kind of over-hard test which seems liable to start a bad habit even in a child who, if guarded from such undue temptation long enough, might never succumb to temptations to steal. Again, an intelligent child of six may have learned to tell the truth and confess small misdemeanours: but if he has done something very naughty and fears severe punishment, he may lie if asked about it and the very breaking of the rule may weaken its hold upon him.

Clearly this is one of the principles of discipline that has to be carefully considered in reference to the timid or 'nervous' child, as his fear of punishment may accentuate the temptation to lie. Personally, for my own children when very young, I adopted the principle at first of giving no penalty for confessed misdeeds: and then I gradually introduced a penalty much milder than if the misdemeanour

tional Development, Social Behaviour and Children's Morals. As to adolescence an old classic is Stanley Hall's two volume *Psychology of Adolescence*; more recent books are Dr. Olive Wheeler's *The Adventure of Youth* and L. S. Hollingworth's *Psychology of the Adolescent*.

had been discovered without confession: for of course, one could not go on indefinitely with no penalty for confessed misdeeds, or they might be indulged in with the consciousness of complete immunity from punishment.

The principle of consistency

The fourth general principle of sound discipline I suggest is that of *consistency* both in rules of conduct and in treatment of misdemeanours. A parent or teacher who on one day condones disobedience or laughs at impertinence, and on another day punishes it severely because he happens to be in a different mood, must expect bewilderment and irregular conduct in a little child and continuous trouble with older ones. In the case of a persistent self-willed little boy, I have seen one serious giving way by a parent throw away the results of improvement slowly gained by previous consistent treatment. One such victory gives hope in every subsequent struggle to the young rebel that he may gain his own way.[1]

Lest this should seem to be supporting the doctrine that the child's will must be 'crushed' may I remind the reader of what was said in the chapter on Repression and Sublimation about the need for success and achievement for the child and even for a due amount of satisfaction of the impulse of self-assertion. There are, however, many occasions, especially in the earliest years, when for the sake of his own bodily health and even safety, a vigorous, active, exploring child may need some penalty to be imposed if he is to be restrained. If yelling loud and long finally worries the mother into letting the child stay up late one night,

[1] Miss C. B. Weill tells a story of a 'well trained child' who was teasing his mother for something she had refused. 'Don't you know that when Mother says *No* she never, never changes her mind?' 'Once you did', was the answer. (*The Behaviour of Young Children of the Same Family*, p. 54.)

after a period of regular hours, the child will almost surely try it on again, and all the gains of previous training may be lost.

The principle of consistency need not, however, be interpreted in a cast-iron or literal way. Circumstances vary, and when the child is old enough to understand their variations, varied treatment may reasonably follow. To take the simple example just used—regular bedtime. A protest against going to bed at the usual time some night when, say, a favourite uncle has called, may reasonably be yielded to—on the ground of the visit, however, and not at threats of a scene.

The principle of consistency would also usually rule out too violent a change in the severity of discipline. Thus one difficult boy, about whom I was consulted, was whipped by his father for the first time at the age of 9;0, and he immediately ran away from home. Even where parents become convinced that their methods of discipline are wrong, it is doubtful whether too sudden a change is advisable. Much, however, will depend on the degree of severity or laxity and on the age and sensitivity of the child. As Professor Burt states, discipline is especially resented by a child who has been pampered in earlier years and then has to be restrained,[1] yet sometimes a sudden and severe check to a violent aggressive boy may be wholesome and necessary.[2]

The need for certainty of detection

Closely connected with this principle of consistency is that of *the inevitability of detection*. History shows that the frequency of crime has declined as penalties have become milder: but some who on this ground advocate greater

---

[1] *The Subnormal Mind*, p. 263.
[2] See the quotation from Burt's book *The Young Delinquent* given later in the chapter on Corporal Punishment, p. 84.

licence for children overlook the fact that the *detection* of crime has become much more certain. In addition to avoiding changes in discipline due to the irrational fluctuation of the moods and impulses of teacher or parent, we must seek so to arrange matters that *if* something is required or forbidden the defaulter shall not have any considerable chance of escaping detection. This is incidentally a reason for avoiding the making of rules of conduct which cannot be adequately supervised. If they can be broken without consequence they will come into contempt. Yet this principle is not one which can cover the whole of conduct. In some types of conduct one must appeal to higher motives to influence behaviour which will not be found out. It is a principle which can only apply to the lower ranges of external conduct.

The need for co-operation

Our fifth principle is that of *co-operation*—between the two parents in the home and between the teachers in the school, and between the school and the home.

We will consider the last two of these pairs briefly here: co-operation of parents in the home, a more difficult and for our purpose usually a more important problem, will be discussed in a separate chapter.

It has already been pointed out in Chapter III that the best results of school training cannot be obtained if the home influences are against it. For the home to make light of ideals of conduct which the school tries to inculcate, will almost inevitably weaken the school's influence. For example, personal habits of cleanliness and tidiness are much harder to establish if the home does not back up the school. Little children sometimes openly protest to the teacher: 'Mother doesn't make me do that.' It is shameful neglect of duty of the parents to shirk the unpleasantness

of restraint and discipline and to try to shift all responsibility for training on to the school. Intellectual interests
fostered at school are also less likely to develop if the home
gives them little or no encouragement. That there should
be mutual understanding of aims is the main justification
for 'parent societies'. Furthermore, in serious cases of
'problem' children, who are being studied and dealt with
either at a Child Guidance Clinic or in the home, the co-
operation of the school in treating the special peculiarities
of each child so far as that is possible, is important.[1]

But the conditions in school are so different from those
at home, and the relationship between child and parent so
different from that between child and teacher (especially
for young children) that we need not expect or desire a
complete similarity between the system of *discipline* at home
and that at school, except so far as the other general principles discussed in these chapters apply to both. Furthermore, where one of the two institutions—the home and the
school—adopts too lax (or too severe) ideals of conduct,
co-operation of the other institution is *not* desirable: it must
do what it can without the help of the other. But the
presence at school of large groups of other children, the usual
absence of the power of a strong appeal to affection (as is
possible for the parent), some need for getting through so
much work in a given period, and yet the occurrence of
play-periods in which no adults are involved—all these make
the conditions of school so different from those of home that
quite another system of rules on minor points of conduct and
of rewards and punishment may be reasonable.[2]

[1] Statistical evidence of the advantages of the help of co-operative
schools in dealing with problem children and the poorer results when
the school problems were not dealt with, are given by C. R. Rogers in
his book, *The Clinical Treatment of the Problem Child*, p. 228.
[2] On the question of discipline and the training of conduct in schools
I would commend the reader to an admirable chapter headed 'Pygmalion

The matter is different, however, when we consider *co-operation between teachers* within the same school. Though lack of co-operation among teachers at school is, I think, less serious than divergence in standards and discipline between parents, yet with young children, especially in the Nursery or perhaps the Infant Schools, marked differences in the standards of conduct required by different teachers are apt to be confusing to the children. If several teachers taking one class at different times are, say, indifferent if the children chatter loudly while doing some handwork, whereas another teacher enjoins quiet or even silence, trouble may ensue for teachers as well as pupils. In some cases children soon discover that teacher A will not allow what B condones; they tend to adapt themselves accordingly, and no great harm may be done if the matter is one largely of the teacher's own preference and not of principle of conduct. The matter is otherwise, however, where serious difficulties occur as to principles, or important methods of discipline. For example, one of my old students went to his first school determined not to use corporal punishment; but he found himself in a minority of one, and after a brave struggle had to give way.

Fortunately on the main ideas as to honest and decent conduct, teachers do not vary much. It is on procedure and methods of discipline that differences are most likely to occur; and the most serious of these, more especially in the elementary schools, is likely to be this very one of corporal punishment. Since this is a matter of lively dispute as regards home discipline too, we may well give it special consideration.

or Procrustes' in Professor Godfrey Thomson's book, *Instinct, Intelligence and Character.*

VIII

THE PROBLEM OF CORPORAL PUNISHMENT

Former abuse of the cane

At Eton in the eighteen-twenties, Dr. Keats 'on heroic occasions was known to have flogged over eighty boys on a single summer day'; and his one 'mellow regret in the evening of his life was that he had not flogged far more'.[1]

Perhaps we may clear the ground a little if we agree first that the excessive and continuous use of the cane or birch in days gone by was not only unnecessary but abhorrent; and that the use even of mild corporal punishment in school or home should at least be rare—a last resort indeed and only for certain types of offence. Such instances as are given of its abuse by Dr. Cyril Norwood[2] and by Mr. L. B. Pekin[3] for example, are revolting in the extreme and show that the use of corporal punishment needs careful supervision.

Fallacious arguments against corporal punishment

Having said so much, however, I would add that the reasons usually given against *all* corporal punishment seem to me as flimsy as some of the other arguments we have dealt with in this book. Here again we meet with similar fallacies. Because flagellation, in some cases (often, and perhaps always abnormal cases), causes sexual excitement, either to the giver or receiver, some argue, like Mr. Pekin himself, as though this were usual or inevitable. Because some persons find during the excitement of the sexual act an impulse to cause pain to the partner, it is argued that all

---

[1] John Morley, *Life of W. E. Gladstone*, Chap. 2.
[2] In *The English Tradition of Education*, Chap. VI.
[3] *Public Schools: their Failure and their Reform*, Chap. III.

pain-causing is accompanied by or even motivated by sex impulse: a logical fallacy even more gross than it would be if we suggested that because the sexual act is accompanied by heavy breathing, therefore all heavy breathing is sexual in its nature!

Though a few autobiographical reports suggest that in some cases corporal punishment may be followed by a profound feeling of humiliation (which we cannot assume is always a bad thing)[1] the assertion that it usually destroys a boy's self-respect lacks evidence. From my own experience, as a boy, of occasional corporal punishment, I can recall no such feeling—though I vividly remember feeling once or twice that it was excessive for the offence (I was once caned severely for talking in class!). Nor did comrades who were caned much oftener than I was show signs of any such humiliation. When I put a question as to a feeling of humiliation or loss of self-respect after corporal punishment to my three boys, who at different periods were at a school where it was used occasionally, the ideas caused considerable amusement. Even the *Report of the Departmental Committee on Corporal Punishment*, though on the whole strongly in favour of the reduction of corporal punishment prescribed by the courts, states, as to the argument that corporal punishment is degrading, 'We have not given much weight to this argument' (p. 59).

The attitude of school children towards caning

One of my former research students, Major K. D. Hopkins, made a careful enquiry into the attitude of school children towards punishments of various kinds—the cane, impositions, detentions, public disgrace, etc. The enquiry

---

[1] Dr. Cyril Norwood indeed says that 'a caning by a Headmaster *should* be regarded as degrading' (*The English Tradition of Education*, p. 73). I imagine he means 'felt to be a disgrace'.

was made in seven schools of different types and included 2,628 children from 8 to 16 years of age. Pupils were promised that no one should see their answers except the investigator. I quote some of the main conclusions about corporal punishment.[1] It should be explained that questions were put as to which of several kinds of punishment would be most effective in certain circumstances (given in the form of short stories), what they (the pupils) would feel like if so punished, which teacher they would like to have, etc.

'Corporal punishment was thought most effective by pupils below the age 12 +. It produced very mixed feelings, of which anger and revengefulness were among the commonest; but, whereas these feelings were so pronounced among the elder children as to make half of them think that a repetition of the offence would occur, among the younger they were acknowledged to be momentary and slight. At 15 + the punishment was declared a failure by 51 per cent of the boys, 22 per cent giving revenge as the reason, while at the age of 10 + only 19 per cent declare it would be a failure, of which 2 per cent gave revenge as the reason. From the age of 14 + downwards an increasing number of boys and girls appeared to consider that a caning was simply a just retribution for the misdeed, wiping it out and leaving the sinner free to repeat the offence or not, as he pleased. In choosing the teacher preferred, approximately 30 per cent of the children chose the severer teachers, particularly the one who used the cane, the deduction being clearly made in many cases that the teacher who could punish efficiently could also teach efficiently and the class would make progress.

---

[1] I have modified one or two sentences for the sake of clarity. A more detailed account of the method and results of the enquiry will be found in Major Hopkins's paper, 'Punishment in Schools' in *The British Journal of Educational Psychology*, Vol. IX, Part I, February 1939.

'Though there was abundant evidence to show that corporal punishment should be avoided as far as possible, and cautiously but effectively administered when to refrain would be a sign of weakness, there was no evidence that it evokes that feeling of physical and spiritual degradation that some of the more enthusiastic opponents of the practice assert. In one of the supplementary questionnaires about 300 children were asked to choose which punishment they would prefer out of the following: (1) two strokes with the cane, (2) five hundred lines to be done at home, (3) one half-day's detention in school. Of the boys 90 per cent, and of the girls 37 per cent, chose the cane, mostly because it was quickly over; 10 per cent of the boys and 60 per cent of the girls chose "lines" and 3 per cent of the girls chose detention. Comparison of the choices made in the main and subsidiary questionnaires suggests that personal convenience (or inconvenience) plays a substantial part in a child's attitude towards punishment. In the main questionnaire the choice was between three punishments that took place during school hours and did not impose extra restraint on the children during their free time: first, the cane which is quickly over; second, the public scolding which took place during lesson time; and third, the kindly lecture which detained the child for only a few minutes. The lecture, which caused the least personal inconvenience, was the most popular choice. In the smaller investigation the choice was between the momentary pain of a sharp caning, the monotony of writing five hundred lines and the restraint of the detention. The popular choice again showed the tendency to prefer the punishment that entailed least inconvenience; the boys chose the cane; the girls, who would probably have to spend much of their evenings at home in any case chose the lines. One very significant similarity appeared in the answers to both questionnaires—no girls above the age of fifteen chose the

F

cane nor, except in a few cases for bullying, did they recommend caning as a punishment. This is in conformity with the widely held belief that adolescent girls have a far greater reverence for their bodies than have boys. Consequently corporal punishment is likely to and, as the records show, does arouse feelings of anger to such an extent as to make it an unsuitable punishment for adolescent girls.'

As to the last mentioned point—corporal punishment for girls—I must confess to feeling a strong revulsion against such a thing, apart from slight slappings in very early years; and even if this is a prejudice due to sex differences, and if a woman may feel less aversion to applying corporal punishment to girls, there seem to me to be good reasons why it should very rarely if ever be used. These reasons lie partly in the nature of the offences for which corporal punishment seems especially suitable, namely such as these young pupils themselves indicate—persistent bullying and physical ill-treatment of others: these are much less frequent among girls. The second reason is that girls are usually more sensitive to reproof and to signs of personal disapproval.

Corporal punishment in the home

As to home discipline, my own view is that with many, probably most, children any form of corporal punishment is unnecessary, except perhaps during the earliest years and in a very mild form before children can really understand what they are doing: when for example a venturesome boy of three or four after repeated prohibitions continues to turn a gas jet up and down, or to do some equally dangerous trick, a smart slap may be needed to make him realize that you are indeed serious. It is (as usual) impossible to generalize here because children vary so enormously in their sensitivity to rebuke. Some are reduced to tears merely by a sharp tone in a beloved mother's rebuke; and to apply the hand to such would not only be unnecessary but probably brutal. In some the fear of physical pain seems so great that a mere threat of corporal punishment may be profoundly disturbing and in some cases possibly itself cause apparent misdemeanours which are merely the consequences of general nervous disturbance.[1] Other children, again, are tough, and after a smacking for some dangerous trick will be friendly, cheery and even cheeky and mischievous again (in some other way) before an hour is passed. To some children other kinds of penalties are enough, such as deprivation of sweets, or being put in the corner. But at least one of my boys was so venturesome and independent and also so cheerful, so much of a Mark Tapley, that such punishment was of little use. I remember when once I had put him in the corner (at about the age of four, mental age then nearly six) shortly after he was let out, he came up to me and said in a most friendly manner: 'Daddy, do you know what I do when you put me in the corner?' 'No, what do you do?' 'I tell God funny stories!'[2]

At a later stage—middle childhood, for the great majority of children I should think that, granted wise management, corporal punishment should not be necessary: but for the boy who will persist in something gravely wrong and especially dangerous to himself or others, and who will not take other penalties seriously, it may be occasionally preferable to a more prolonged form of punishment.

For the really difficult rebellious child with a threatening

---

[1] Threats of whipping for bed-wetting, for example, seem to be particularly futile. On the varied causes (physical and psychological) and treatment of enuresis see *Child Psychiatry* by Dr. Leo Kanner (London, 1935); also Professor Burt's article 'The Incidence of Neurotic Symptoms among Evacuated School Children', *British Journal of Educational Psychology*, 1940, Vol. X, p. 14.

[2] This boy, I may add, paddled on the beach at Dunkirk while the bombs were still falling!

to complete revolt or bullying or cruelty, I think one may be driven to occasional corporal punishment; but this should be in conjunction with other measures and only after a serious attempt to understand and deal with any environmental causes of the trouble. It does seem possible that as the mildness of some recent penalties gets known among our venturesome or lawless youths, they may become ineffective as deterrents. A social worker at a Child Guidance Clinic recently heard one boy asking a friend who had been to a reformatory school, what it was like. 'Oh! it's all right,' was the reply, 'you get comics to read in bed.' A teacher in one of my classes told me that one of his boys recently boasted to him that a magistrate (of a children's court before which he had been summoned) told him he should 'express himself'. Professor Burt, though he thinks that the corporal punishment of juvenile delinquents usually does more harm than good (N.B.—those punished are usually adolescents and considerably older than the children we have in mind at the moment) nevertheless states a case for its effectiveness in certain instances:

'Brutality to other children, gross cruelty to animals, endangering the lives of railway passengers by putting obstructions on the line, these are obviously transgressions where the birch may prove an efficacious means of bringing home to the offender himself the sharp significance of pain. . . .' 'I can, in fact, cite more than one example of an older lad, too strong for his father to thrash, where the same penalty, informally applied by a burly policeman, has had a final and deterrent result. Moreover, a rare and occasional birching, if it does not reform the one boy birched, may yet overawe a dozen others whose nature it is to respond to fear rather than to clemency.'[1]

It will be recalled that, as found by Major Hopkins,

[1] See C. Burt, *The Young Delinquent*, pp. 121-2.

school pupils usually thought that corporal punishment was especially the right penalty for bullying and physical violence; and this fits in with the findings of J. Piaget that, as children get older, the principle of reciprocity in punishment replaces that of mere vindictiveness, in their ideas of the basis of punishment.[1]

[1] See *The Moral Judgment of the Child*, Chap. 3.

IX

PARENTS AND HOME DISCIPLINE

ONE OF THE chief problems in the bringing up of children in the home is that of *co-operation between parents* in matters of discipline. Such co-operation is, I think, more important than co-operation between teachers, which we considered at the end of Chapter VII; certainly it is a more delicate problem to discuss, but we must face it.

I doubt whether many educationists troubled much about this problem in the days of Victorian discipline, though the severe parent would no doubt usually be perturbed by the laxity of the other, and the tender one would be upset by her mate's severity. In more recent studies of child psychology, and especially of problem children, such division between the parents has become a prominent element, and in the literature of the subject one constantly finds complaints that one parent is too severe and the other over-indulgent. In one enquiry about the home life of juvenile delinquents, it was found that in 41 per cent of the 133 families studied, the parents disagreed about the discipline of their children 'especially of the delinquent' child.[1] One of the difficulties in addressing ourselves to parents is this: that (as with the problem of co-operation between a school with high ideals of conduct, and a home with low ideals) the yielding of one parent to co-operate with the other, or a compromise in the standard of conduct to be required or in the degree of discipline to be imposed, is not necessarily the best solution. To an omniscient psychological judge, one of the two parents might be completely right: or

[1] W. Healey and A. F. Bronner, *New Light on Delinquency and its Treatment*, p. 30 (Yale Univ. Press, 1936).

indeed the more severe of two parents may still be too lax—and in another home the more indulgent one may be still too severe.

It is not difficult to see several unfortunate consequences likely to happen where there is a great divergence between the parents in the control of the children: but we should recognize that even marked difference in the standards and discipline of the parents does not necessarily mean that the children will prove undisciplined or difficult. I have known personally a number of families in which such differences between the parents, and very decided ones, have existed: and yet in some of these families all the children, and in others all except one, have developed well. We are indeed reminded of the conclusion already reached in considering all kinds of broken, drunken or ill-disciplined homes, namely, that the characters of some children survive the most unfavourable environment, while with some the results depend much more on the training they receive. The difficulties resulting from a clash of standards and methods between the parents are likely to appear especially with the child with excessive innate assertiveness, extreme selfishness or other serious defects—in short, with the 'difficult child'. Such a one will naturally tend to think that the indulgent parent is right, and the more severe one wrong and unjust.

The meaning of 'home discipline'

As this section relates entirely to home discipline, it may be well to point out the very varied aspects of such discipline. Perhaps 'control' would be a better word for some of them. Some confident prescribers for the home treatment of children seem to have had little experience in the actual bringing up of children in the home. In the first place, some write as though the home could and should be run entirely for the children, ignoring the needs of the parents. It is indeed to the advantage of the children themselves that the mother should not be over-wearied with tending them, and that the father after a hard day's work should find some peace and quiet in his home. (May I recall that I have already stressed the importance of children having some place and some times in the day when they can 'let themselves go'.)

Second, from babyhood there must inevitably be constant restraint of many actions for the child's own safety and well-being. In infancy there must be refusal of unsuitable food and restraint from too dangerous actions. This caution is easily overdone, no doubt, and the child made nervous by unnecessary suggestions. We always allowed our children to take slight risks in climbing trees, etc., in the garden, and found the excellent 'heads' for heights they thus developed to be of value on at least one critical occasion. Still, there must be many occasions for the restraint of some venturesome spirits.

Neglect as to clothing—going out inadequately protected from rain or cold, and many other matters affecting health, must be firmly dealt with; and as the child grows up these things cannot always be seen to by the mother; so the child himself must be usually held responsible, and penalties for neglect are better than repeated minor ailments. Careless spoiling of his own clothing or destruction of house property must in most homes be discouraged for reasons of economy. And so in many ways, apart from any vicious tendencies, an active independent child may need repeated correction and sometimes reproof and even minor penalties, if his own welfare is to be safeguarded and if conditions in the home are to be tolerable for others.

The consequences of different standards of two parents

In all these matters, after the first two or three years of babyhood, co-operation between the parents is important. If one parent who tries to set a reasonable standard in these matters is opposed by indifference or carelessness of the other parent, obvious enough to cause encouragement of the child in his neglect, then the child will naturally tend to follow the one whose ideas fit in best with his own inclinations of the moment, and the task of training is made much harder. This is especially so with the 'difficult' child, because the lenient parent is so apt to feel that the child's tantrums or the youth's revolts and misdemeanours must be yielded to and condoned lest discipline should cause more intense resistance: and this very indulgence sets a standard for the child against which he contrasts the firmness of the other parent, who appears all the more severe and unjust by this very contrast.

This danger of differences between parents as to standards and discipline has often been stressed by writers on problem children: but there is one consequence of such differences to the parent who undertakes the main burden of discipline which is apt to be overlooked. One such father well known to me as a devoted 'family man', and thoughtful beyond the average, wrote about this point as follows: 'One of the chief sources of unhappiness in my life has been having to do nearly all the discipline since the children were two or three years old. Their mother would, often with great unselfishness, do far too much for them and often approve things bad for them for the sake of the child's immediate enjoyment. Even when young the children seemed to absorb the constant subtle (unintentional) suggestions from her that my own attempts to restrain over-indulgence or unhealthy habits, or to check inconsiderate and selfish behaviour, were unnecessary and interfering. I am sure the affection of the children for me was affected by all this. Often I have longed to do some indulging myself when already there had been too much. I am pretty sure my wife would have become a household drudge to certain of the children if I had been long absent from home. But all this has meant reconciling myself to having from the children much less affection than I might have had.'

In such a case, however unselfish and devoted the lenient or lax parent may be, it is unfair to leave all the burden of restraint on the other, and so be able to be more indulgent because of that very discipline which is shirked and even openly disapproved of.

Usually, no doubt, the various aspects of control are shared: the mother will be firm about proper feeding and other health matters and will see to the economy of clothing, the father perhaps will see that school work is not neglected, and check extravagances in the bigger items of expenditure: both will join when serious offences are committed. The unfairness arises when (as apparently in the case just quoted) all these aspects of discipline devolve largely on the one parent; when that parent must do nearly all the restraining and the other all the indulging; when the latter also talks as though any expenditure can be undertaken if only father (or mother) will agree; or as though doing the homework is of trivial importance and that no attractive social engagement should be sacrificed for it.

The child will soon become aware of such differences, without any open dispute by the parents. Repeated silence by parent B when parent A reproves a child for a fault, or even worse, the immediate following of A's reproof by a pleasant remark by B to the child on some entirely different subject and in a particularly sympathetic tone: these will make the child feel at once that B is 'on his side'. But it is even worse of course when there is open dispute and B denounces A's action in the presence of the child. At the least the parents should discuss their different views as to the children's conduct and discipline in private, and try not to confuse the mind of the child or to make their own conflict clear by open dispute. Of course all this also refers to other relatives who are liable to criticize the discipline of parents openly at times. One mother who consulted me recently about a very difficult boy, told me that when she reproved the boy for misdemeanours the grandmother would reply openly in the boy's presence that he would be 'all right' if his mother would leave him alone. Is it any wonder that when he was finally punished for a serious offence he ran away to his grandmother's home?

When there are so many varying degrees of difference between the parents' ideas and so many doubtful questions of good and bad discipline, it is difficult to do much more than point out to parents who differ strongly such possible consequences as are mentioned above. But there is one question that the lenient or indulgent partner may profitably put to himself (or herself) at times, namely, 'What should I have to do if my wife (or husband) abandoned all attempts at discipline or even had always left it to me?' Alas, even that may only bring to the blind parent, infatuated with her child's supreme perfection the conviction that the troublesome child might have been even better with the more lax treatment. It is such parents I had in view when I remarked in the first chapter that the surprising assertion that the boy's worst enemy is his mother might have had some truth in it if the speaker had added 'in some cases'.

The mother more usually the lax disciplinarian

Although the father is not always the more severe disciplinarian and although the mother is often, perhaps usually, the more *constant* or frequent disciplinarian—if only because she usually spends so much more time with the children in the home—nevertheless it is usually the mother who does that extreme spoiling of the child which is liable to make him a 'difficult' child.[1] Miss Witmer, for example, in the enquiry among problem children already quoted, found twenty-one cases in which the child was 'an outlet for the

[1] In an enquiry among about 80 graduate students some years ago I found that the father was more frequently the more severe disciplinarian among the boys and the mother among the girls. (Reported in *The New Psychology of the Unconscious*, p. 88.) In a more recent enquiry by anonymous questionnaire, among men and women graduates, I drew a distinction between the more *severe* and the more *constant* (frequent) disciplinarian and also between different age periods, with the following results. It will be seen that the father was much more frequently the severe disciplinarian for boys over 5 and even for adolescent girls.

Ages	More severe disciplinarian		More constant disciplinarian	
	Father	Mother	Father	Mother
MEN				
1–5	18	14	2½	23
6–10	22½	10½	8	25
11–15	23	7	10	15
16–20	14½	3½	11	8
WOMEN				
1–5	10	18	6	24
6–10	17½	14½	1	30
11–15	18	10	2½	26½
16–20	13	8	1	19½

N.B.—Numbers do not always balance because in some alternatives students could give no report; and as they grew older some children lost father or mother and no further reports were made. Others said they had no discipline in the period 16–20 years.

mother's emotions'; but she gives not even one similar case for the fathers.

Burt in his discussions of juvenile delinquents speaks several times of the over-indulgent mother, but I do not recollect such a reference to fathers.[1] Some of the psycho-analysts, as the result of the frequency of spoiling by the mother, have devised the special term 'Mother-complex'; and there is considerable agreement that the absence of so many fathers from home during the last war, and the laxity and indulgence of the mother, was one cause of increasing trouble among adolescents.

If indeed the general view is right (which also is strongly asserted by McDougall) that the protective instinct and affection towards the child is usually stronger in the mother than in the father, then we should expect that it would also be found more frequently in an extreme and unbalanced degree.[2] In enquiries about the homes of problem children amazing stories of over-mothering have come to light, for example of children who insist on sleeping with the mother till the age of ten or over; of children of that age whom the mother coddles and still helps to dress; of adolescents from whom the mother takes over all responsibility and whom she indulges and keeps in her company whenever possible, so that some of the less sociable and more selfish of the young

[1] In his comprehensive study of backward children Burt singles out the 'efficiency of the mother' as 'the one feature in the home which shows the closest relation to the child's school progress'. *The Backward Child*, p. 133.

[2] It is interesting to note that great extremes also appear in the 'mother instinct' in the higher apes. Chimpanzee mothers according to a high authority vary extremely; some are 'pronouncedly conservative', some 'markedly radical'. Infant independence is sometimes encouraged and sometimes discouraged. R. M. Yerkes and M. I. Tomlin, 'Mother—infant relations in Chimpanzee', *Journal of Comparative Psychology*, XX, 1925. Some mother-monkeys have been known to persist in carrying about with them a dead infant for several weeks after its death.

people become too dependent on the mother for the rest of their young manhood or young womanhood at least, and cannot form new lasting interests or attachments. Such 'fixations' of child on mother—and we may add of mother on child—may be partly the cause and partly the result of unsatisfactory relations with the husband, and a vicious circle is apt to be set up. At other times the situation may be due to the coincidence in one family of (a) a child unusually selfish or with specially strong tendencies to crave protection and devotion, and (b) a mother whose 'mothering' instinct is abnormally strong and continues to function towards a child when he has long passed the age which needs it. As McDougall points out, the lessening of tender solicitude as the child grows into young manhood is a perfectly natural consequence of the fact that, as the child grows up, he gradually loses those qualities which appeal directly to the parental instinct.[1] After that stage affection is more dependent upon the qualities the young people actually show; though with the great majority of parents, there continues much of the parental instinctive impulse even after the childhood needs are over. In some cases such impulses may be abnormally strong and excessively prolonged, and a mother would fain carry all the burdens of her child who is no longer a child, and who ought to be fending for himself.

When this extreme mothering comes even in middle childhood, the situation may in some cases be saved by sending the child away to boarding school. It is significant that Dr. C. Rogers, in his survey of the effects of institutional treatment for problem children, concludes that, though usually it seems inferior to foster homes, it is preferable to a foster home for the 'spoiled child'.[2] Where such removal is impossible or is resisted by the parent, the only hope in

[1] *Outline of Psychology*, p. 139.
[2] *Clinical Treatment of the Problem Child*, p. 138.

such extreme cases seems to be for some mutual friend and wise observer to seek to show, as impartially as possible, the serious consequences to the child itself. The mother's affection may be strong enough to enable her to try gradually to free both herself and her child from the too close bond. This involves intelligence and self-criticism, but the experience of social workers and psychologists who have tackled the problem shows that while there are some failures there are also some successes. Any candid friend who seeks to help, however, must take a considerable risk of antagonizing the mother who continues blind to her spoiling of the child.

X

CONCLUSION

IN CONCLUDING this little book I am acutely conscious of the fact that it is only a very short treatment of a large and difficult subject—of several difficult subjects indeed. I can only hope that it may serve as a warning against too hurried acceptance of some modern theories, and as a guide to further and more substantial studies.

In a short critical and controversial treatment like this it is necessary to pass lightly over many important ideas, when these are accepted by all parties. Yet there is a danger that the reader will get the impression that, because much less space is being given to those ideas, less importance is attached to them. I should like therefore briefly to guard against two or three possible wrong impressions.

Right treatment reduces the need for discipline

Recent fallacies about discipline have consisted largely in the denial of the need for any restraining discipline and of the efficiency of even mild corporal punishment under any circumstances. In combating these ideas I have already stressed (especially in the sections on sublimation) the need for providing positive and suitable activities for the natural impulses of the child; but perhaps it should be emphasized here that the great majority of children need little corrective discipline (at least after infancy) given the means of congenial activities in the home, and provided they have school studies which appeal to the natural interests and activities of childhood, under teachers who have a genuine understanding of, and sympathy with, children.

No parent should conclude that his child is a 'difficult'

one unless, without success, he has tried rewards as well as penalties, praise as well as reproof, and until he has provided ample means for congenial activities appropriate to the age and special interests of the child, as we said in Chapter VII. The idea that discipline must largely consist of 'don'ts' is wholly wrong; the ideal is to avoid unnecessary prohibitions. Mischief, with the majority of children, is no doubt usually a substitute for the craving for interesting and even exciting experiences. I write these words a day after seeing a mother and her little girls on the Malvern Hills. The girls were constantly running about the hillside, of which the slope at that part was so slight that at the worst the children could only suffer a slight bumping for a few feet if they rolled over. Yet the mother was constantly crying out 'Don't run, Mary,' or 'Come here, Joan,' etc.

The constant unnecessary checking of children of which this example is typical, is as deplorable as that laxity and fear of all restraining, which has been criticized in this book. It does not, however, need the same type of systematic criticism because it is not based on professed psychological grounds, as are the theories we have been concerned with.

It should, however, be stressed that it is a healthy sign if children are constantly active and seeking new experiences; and it is foolish to check such impulses unnecessarily, for it is quite likely that, if so checked, they will tend to find even less desirable channels. The ideal indeed is that appropriate means for activities and interests of every legitimate kind should actually be provided for the child. This cannot be left to the unguided intuition or 'common sense' of the parent, which too frequently is apt to err either in the way just indicated—perpetual 'don'ts' and restrictions, or in feeble yieldings to protest and temper. It must be realized that the bringing up even of normal children requires careful thought and planning, which leads us to our next point.

G

The training of children a difficult art

The provision of suitable activities for the child needs some careful study of children, and perhaps consultation with teachers or others with a wider knowledge of children of the particular age, supplemented by some reading of the psychology of normal children. Some parents are puzzled when they buy expensive toys for a child and it is not satisfied. It may be that he craves for more 'natural' activities—the climbing of trees, a dip in the river, animals to care for, or for play with children of his own age; or for material with which he can make things, e.g. Plasticine, wood and tools, etc., etc. The selection and provision of these by the parent at the appropriate time is no easy matter (especially in towns) and deserves careful thought, observation, and experiment. No one who has read this little book will conclude that I think the right treatment of a 'difficult' child to be an easy thing: the very term indeed indicates the opposite; but neither is the bringing up of a child so that he will not develop into a difficult child, an easy thing. True, I have concluded (in Chapter II) that a certain number of children will develop well even if badly brought up: but it was there also suggested that the greater proportion of children are of that intermediate type who are likely to become 'difficult' in adverse conditions. If so, both probability and wise caution would suggest that the parent should assume that his child is of that intermediate type, and that his development depends on the training he receives.

As indicated earlier (especially in Chapters I and II) the parent need not be unduly alarmed at occasional outbursts and troublesome periods; but if serious difficulties do develop he should not hesitate to consult others, and to learn from every possible source, more of child psychology. For this purpose some discussion and study groups are useful, or the parents' meetings held at some schools, or the study of books of the type I mention later. Finally, if the child seems in danger of growing beyond parental control, or otherwise appears too different from the normal, an early consultation with a competent child psychologist, or a visit to a Guidance Clinic, may be advisable.

These recommendations for planning, study, and consultation, are, of course, addressed to the more educated and intelligent parents; they can hardly apply to large numbers of parents of children in elementary schools. Here comes the value of the full and varied activities of the modern infant, junior, and senior schools. Especially is the Nursery School a boon for those children and parents in poor homes where, even if outside work did not claim much of the mother's time, she has no means of providing for such activities, and so often has little idea as to how to bring up her own little ones. No doubt the more troublesome children tend to be brought most frequently to the Nursery School, but even so I have been impressed by the number of children who, reports show, are being wrongly treated at home; and especially of those who are said to be difficult at home, but who are happy, active and decently behaved at school. Thus Augustus, aged 3½ years (described in Chapter III, p. 29), was reported by his mother to be 'a little devil' at home: 'yesterday he would not let his dad have his tea'. My daughter's account of him was that he was a 'lovely boy if you treat him rightly, with a keen sense of humour'. Another boy, George H., aged 2½ years, an only child, was reported very difficult at home; his mother could not manage him. At school he appeared 'a little saint'. 'He cried first at rest time, but tried to repress his sobs when I appealed to him not to disturb the others; very sensitive to reproach; I think the mother expects the impossible.' Other children are evidently completely spoiled, some being allowed to

*

dominate the home. Others are treated most stupidly; e.g. foolish things are said about them in their presence—that they will not do as they are told, or words revealing the mother's lack of affection for them. Since beginning this chapter I have heard of one mother so foolish as to tell her boy a lie, which she knew he would learn the same day was a lie. He was a new boy (age about four years) at the nursery school, and greatly disliked going to bed for the after-dinner sleep. When he wept about it at home, his mother (as she confessed) to pacify him told him they would not be going to bed that day—and repeated the story several days. (This boy, by the way, when my daughter said, 'Don't cry, Tommy, you're not going to bed till after dinner, and you have all the morning to play', said amid sobs, 'Well, when you do get the beds out for us to go to bed, do you mind if I cry then?')

I need hardly stress, however, this fact, so well known to most school teachers and social workers, of the ignorance and foolishness of so many even well-meaning parents as to the bringing up of their children. Many of such parents can learn something by that direct contact with the teachers which the nursery school brings; others may be incapable of learning much. Here again is some further justification of the distinction I drew in Chapter III of the much greater need of the Nursery School for children with certain types of parents and homes; and here also are reasons why the above remarks about the careful study of the problem of bringing up children can only apply to a certain proportion of parents.

The positive results of child psychology

There is a second erroneous impression I would like to safeguard against. In the early chapters I have repeatedly stressed the limitations of our knowledge on certain points in the social psychology of early childhood and especially about the difficult child. This was necessary to combat the dogmatism of some who speak so confidently of this and that having been '*proved*', with no evidence that justifies more than a surmise, if that.

It should, however, be emphasized that, as I have occasionally indicated, there is a substantial body of well-established psychological facts and principles which apply to children as well as to adults, and a further large range of well-established facts about the development of normal children. These largely refer to mental development, the processes of learning and remembering, and the measurement of intelligence; but the development of interests and the study of fundamental impulses are also well represented. The study of such wider psychological topics is strongly recommended to parents and teachers, and I give below references to a small selection of books. A study of some of these will provide a steadying background of knowledge, and this will serve as a further safeguard against that too ready acceptance of superficial psychological doctrines which it has been one of the purposes of this little book to combat.

References for further reading

As to special topics related to problem children the reader will find ample references already given; for more general reading as to social development in early childhood and adolescence he is referred to the footnote in Chapter VII, p. 71.

To the books there mentioned may be added, for the study of development in the first three or four years, A. Gesell's *The Mental Growth of the Pre-school Child*, and W. Stern's *Psychology of Early Childhood*.

An excellent introduction to Educational Psychology is Godfrey Thomson's *Instinct, Intelligence and Character* (George Allen and Unwin).

The study of the psychology of childhood is apt to be incomplete and superficial if the student does not read some books on more general psychology. For this R. H. Thouless's *General and Social Psychology* (University Tutorial Press) can be confidently recommended. As to Social Psychology, the best introduction, in my opinion, is still W. McDougall's *Social Psychology* (Methuen). McDougall subsequently modified his views somewhat on instincts in man, but the chief change was that he changed the label 'Instinct' to that of 'Innate Propensities'. McDougall's later views are given in his more comprehensive book *The Energies of Man* (Methuen).

As to experimental psychology, a comprehensive book is that by Mary Collins and J. Drever, entitled *Experimental Psychology* (Methuen). Experimental work forms the main substance also of Wynn Jones's *Theory and Practice of Psychology* (Macmillan). Those parts of experimental psychology which have a special bearing on education, are dealt with in the present writer's *Introduction to Experimental Psychology* (University Tutorial Press). C. W. Valentine's *Intelligence Tests for Children* (Methuen) gives tests for the ages from 1;6 to 11;0, with full instructions. In the Third Edition tests have been added for the years 12;0 to 15;0.

APPENDIX

IN THIS appendix are given some notes and more recent references to a number of points bearing on topics discussed in the chapters mentioned.

Chapter I. As to emotional symptoms and behaviour in *unselected* school children, see article by Jean Cummings, 'The incidence of emotional symptoms in school children' (*Brit. Jour. of Educ. Psych.* Vol. XIV, 1944, p. 151). This article reveals what a large proportion of ordinary school children between 2 and 7 years of age show what some people would regard as 'problem' behaviour.

In a sound article on 'A Follow-up Study of Emotional Symptoms in School Children' (*Brit. Jour. of Educ. Psych.*, Vol. XVI, 1946), Mrs. Cummings reports that of children between 2;0 and 5;0, 87 per cent. were improved after an interval of 18 months. Of the children of 5;0 and over, 53 per cent. were improved after 18 months. There was especially marked improvement as regards 'anti-social behaviour' and 'nervous habits': much less improvement as to 'day-dreaming' or 'lack of concentration'.

Chapter I, p. 11. A detailed report of the author's enquiry as to the Oedipus Complex and the attitude of infants towards parents is given in his *Psychology of Early Childhood* (Methuen, 3rd edition, 1946) Chapter XVII, 'Affection for parents and the supposed Oedipus Complex'. See also Chapter XVIII, 'The development of sex and sex-interests in infancy'.

Chapter II. A fuller discussion as to innate differences and their effect on behaviour will be found in *The Psychology of Early Childhood* (3rd edition, pp. 19–24).

Chapter III, pp. 25–27. As to changes in behaviour in 'normal' children see Jean D. Cummings' article referred to above in the *Brit. Jour. of Educ. Psych.* Vol. XVI, 1946.

Chapter III, p. 28. As to the influence of broken homes, see the outline of 'An Enquiry into the Influence of Broken Homes on the Maladjustment of Children' (*Brit. Jour. of Educ. Psych.* Vol. XVI, 1946, p. 45), by Jean Adam. She concluded that the influences of the disruption of the home on children may be much less than has been commonly assumed. In about 60 per cent. of the homes from which the problem children came, parental disharmony was a major incidental factor.

As to the influence of a broken home see also 'The Problem Child and his Environment', by H. Banister and M. Ravden (*Brit.*

Jour. of Psych. Vol. XXXIV, 1944). This is a study of 112 children referred to a clinic.

A report on 93 'normal' children from similar schools is given by the same authors in an article on 'The Environment and the Child' (*Brit. Jour. of Psych.* Vol. XXXV, 1945). They found a significant difference between the number of problem children and normal children in broken homes, but suggest that to a considerable extent this may be due to 'the psychological effects of instability in the parents'. They found *'inadequate or improper discipline'* in 66 per cent. of the cases of problem children.

The proportion of *only children* was the same in both groups.

Chapter VI. Interesting material bearing on the relation between unsatisfactory school work (especially truancy) and later maladjustment will be found in an article by Clifford Lummis on 'The Relation of School Attendance to Employment Records, Army Conduct, and Performance in Tests' (*Brit. Jour. of Educ. Psych.* Vol. XVI, 1946).

INDEX

As the Contents Pages give a full guide to the main subjects, this index is largely confined to names and special topics

PRINTED IN GREAT BRITAIN BY
UNWIN BROTHERS LIMITED, LONDON AND WOKING

For Product Safety Concerns and Information please contact our EU
representative GPSR@taylorandfrancis.com
Taylor & Francis Verlag GmbH, Kaufingerstraße 24, 80331 München, Germany

* 9 7 8 1 1 3 8 8 9 9 3 8 4 *